QUICK
leadership

QUICK

leadership

Build Trust, Navigate Change,
and Cultivate
Unstoppable Teams

Selena Rezvani

WILEY

Published by John Wiley & Sons, Inc., Hoboken, New Jersey.
Published simultaneously in Canada.

The manufacturer's authorized representative according to the EU General Product Safety Regulation is Wiley-VCH GmbH, Boschstr. 12, 69469 Weinheim, Germany, e-mail: Product_Safety@wiley.com.

Trademarks: Wiley and the Wiley logo are trademarks or registered trademarks of John Wiley & Sons, Inc. and/or its affiliates in the United States and other countries and may not be used without written permission. All other trademarks are the property of their respective owners. John Wiley & Sons, Inc. is not associated with any product or vendor mentioned in this book.

Limit of Liability/Disclaimer of Warranty: While the publisher and the authors have used their best efforts in preparing this work, including a review of the content of the work, neither the publisher nor the authors make any representations or warranties with respect to the accuracy or completeness of the contents of this work and specifically disclaim all warranties, including without limitation any implied warranties of merchantability or fitness for a particular purpose. No warranty may be created or extended by sales representatives, written sales materials or promotional statements for this work. The fact that an organization, website, or product is referred to in this work as a citation and/or potential source of further information does not mean that the publisher and authors endorse the information or services the organization, website, or product may provide or recommendations it may make. This work is sold with the understanding that the publisher is not engaged in rendering professional services. The advice and strategies contained herein may not be suitable for your situation. You should consult with a specialist where appropriate. Further, readers should be aware that websites listed in this work may have changed or disappeared between when this work was written and when it is read. Neither the publisher nor authors shall be liable for any loss of profit or any other commercial damages, including but not limited to special, incidental, consequential, or other damages.

For general information on our other products and services or for technical support, please contact our Customer Care Department within the United States at (800) 762-2974, outside the United States at (317) 572-3993 or fax (317) 572-4002.

Wiley also publishes its books in a variety of electronic formats. Some content that appears in print may not be available in electronic formats. For more information about Wiley products, visit our web site at www.wiley.com.

Library of Congress Cataloging-in-Publication Data is Available:

ISBN: 9781394339792 (Paperback)
ISBN: 9781394339808 (ePub)
ISBN: 9781394339815 (ePDF)

Cover Design: Wiley
Cover Image: © Selena Rezvani
Printed and bound by CPI Group (UK) Ltd, Croydon, CR0 4YY
C9781394339792_240925

For the leader who's juggling metrics, morale, and a meeting that definitely could've been an email—this is for you.

CONTENTS

INTRODUCTION

The reality of managing today? It's a tough gig. There are employees who've quiet-quit. Go-getters who are impatient to move up. People who are there for the "good-enough" job. And let's not forget the endless pile of deliverables that seems to multiply like laundry. Leadership today is the ultimate plate-spin—you're part coach, part crisis manager, part hype squad, and sometimes even part human whiteboard.

And if you're like most leaders, you're probably looking for ways to manage it all without losing your mind (or your sense of humor). Because let's face it, some days it probably feels like you're one BCC away from launching into a full-on eye twitch. And who'd blame you if the next overly urgent deadline made you consider starting a new career altogether?

If you barely have a moment to catch your breath (just pressure to keep pace with the next thing), no wonder you feel overwhelmed, trying to stay on top of constantly shifting demands. Organizational changes, rapid technological advances, and evolving employee expectations—it's a lot. And here's the kicker: It's only going to get more complicated.

Instead of pushing through, let's try something different. Because no matter how much we normalize rushing, urgency, and the endless pressure to perform, leadership today is about centering what truly matters: *people fundamentals*. It's about focusing on everyday habits that build trust and human connection, habits that address our core needs.

Strong leadership thrives on a steady foundation where your team feels valued, heard, and supported. By consistently showing up with authenticity, empathy, and clarity, you can foster the kind of environment where both you and your team can flourish, no matter the pressures or challenges at hand. And that's not some motivational fluff! This is about practical, actionable tools that can make leadership sustainable, energizing, and effective.

And I know with everything in your planner that might sound like a stretch, but trust me—you're fully capable of it. You don't need a glittery magic wand or to work yourself into the ground either. What you need is a clear roadmap that guides you toward the kind of leadership where you don't just survive the day—you actively help people speak up, take initiative, and do their best work. I'm not asking you to pull off miracles here. I am asking you to take control of what you can, be the steady hand, the clear voice, and the reason your team wants to keep going.

For sure, the expectations are high, and the stakes can feel like they keep getting raised every time you turn around. But here's something I want you to keep in mind: you don't have to carry the weight of it all by yourself. Many leaders are facing the same struggles *right now*—managing performance challenges, cross-team friction, and the constant push to do more with less.

That's where *Quick Leadership* comes in—designed to bring managers together around real-world strategies, relatable tools, and the kind of support that actually sticks.

You may know me from my work as an executive coach, author, and workplace culture consultant. I've been in the trenches evaluating workplaces, from the best in the world to those struggling. I've seen firsthand what works and what doesn't. I've also coached and trained thousands of emerging leaders, and yes, I've been promoted, managed others, been managed, and even been laid off (yep, I've seen both sides of that coin). I've had wonderful managers, toxic ones, and everything in between. But here's the thing: No matter how many surveys, 360 assessments, or focus groups I've conducted on leadership and culture, I've noticed that leaders tend to over-index on managing performance, and neglect the people side: cultivating trust and mutual respect.

Instead of focusing solely on crushing your performance metrics, we'll dig into how you can build a workplace culture that's grounded in connection, open communication, and a sense of shared ownership. And you don't need to be an infallible superhero or perfectly polished role model to do it! In fact, as a self-proclaimed "eat cake before dinner" person (yup, that's me), I know that effective leadership isn't rooted in perfection. It's grounded in flexibility and bringing a bit of humor along the way. It thrives on being real and using your natural strengths as a leader while learning from your inevitable missteps and challenges.

If you're reading this, it's clear you care about being the kind of leader who drives results, inspires your team, and creates an environment where people can thrive. But you're probably also wondering how on earth you can do all that while keeping yourself (and your team) sane. Perhaps these sound familiar:

- How do I motivate a team when morale is low?
- How do I set boundaries when expectations are totally unrealistic?
- How do I keep my cool when it feels like I'm about to snap?
- How do I encourage my team to prioritize their well-being when it feels so challenging to do it myself?

I can tell you you're not the only one asking those questions. Leaders everywhere are trying to figure out how to keep teams motivated when burnout is looming, how to manage up without losing yourself, and how to accept ambiguity when what you're craving is certainty. It's easy to feel like you're not doing enough, like you're missing the mark, or, worse, that you're falling behind.

But vulnerability is part of this gig. It's about embracing the constant learning that comes with the role. You might feel buried under a mountain of tasks, urgent demands, and tough decisions but *ding-ding-ding!* that's exactly when the opportunity to grow as a leader arises. The best leaders aren't those who never get overwhelmed, but those who know how to lean into discomfort, ask for feedback, and adjust their approach. They recognize that they don't need to have it all figured out, and instead focus on staying flexible, learning from missteps, and finding new ways to move forward, no matter how uncertain the road ahead may seem.

I've seen this firsthand. As a coach and consultant, I've worked with leaders from all different industries, and I can tell you this: Leadership is never about having a set of foolproof solutions. The most effective leaders iterate and experiment. They expect some of their hypotheses to be wrong and they learn from their mistakes. They stay adaptable and resourceful, even when the path isn't clear. More than that, they build teams that can do the same: teams empowered to take on challenges and grow alongside them. So don't think you have to figure it all out alone.

This book is about helping you cultivate that mindset.

Quick Leadership offers you practical advice that speaks to the everyday realities of leadership—in a format that's short and sweet, *because you don't have a lifetime to learn this stuff!* Whether you're managing a small team or trying to wrangle a global workforce, the goal is simple: to help you thrive, not just survive, and, by extension, to help your team do the same.

One of the biggest challenges today is managing employees with different expectations and motivations. Some are seeking purpose, fulfillment, and meaningful work. Others prefer a more straightforward approach: coming to work, doing a job, and not feeling like every task is tied to a higher mission. (As one Gen Z professional recently told me, "I do my job and go home. Work is only one small part of my identity.") Balancing these different work expectations is no easy feat but it's absolutely possible. This book will help you meet diverse needs and lead a team that delivers.

And you'll see too how leadership requires a healthy dose of *self*-management. If you're constantly burned out, stressed, and scrambling, your team will feel that energy, too. That's why we'll dive into managing your own well-being as part of the leadership equation. Because leadership shouldn't be a marathon of misery. We'll explore strategies for managing stress, taking breaks, and maintaining perspective so you're not communicating to your team "You should go home now" while you secretly stay until dawn.

Here's what you can expect from your investment of time in this book: actionable strategies based on science and research, practical experience, and real-world advice, so you have tools that help you lead better, starting *today. (No endless theories or abstract concepts that sound good in a lecture but leave you wondering how to apply them!)* We'll cover:

- **Delegating in ways that empower your team, helping *them* grow while you tackle the bigger picture:** Know when to lead and when to trust your team to take the reins. Building trust by giving others ownership takes time and consistency, but when done right, it reinforces accountability, trust, and loyalty.

- **Navigating constant change from a calm center, so you're not just reacting, you're leading:** The pace of change can feel overwhelming, but you can stay grounded by developing a mindset that anticipates change and adapts quickly. This means creating space for feedback, allowing concerns to be heard, and involving people in the process.

- **Creating a culture where your team feels safe to speak up, share ideas, and even fail forward, so they can take ownership and solve problems confidently:** When your team knows they can take risks, raise concerns, and make mistakes without facing negative consequences, they'll feel empowered to step up and contribute, giving you more insights and time to tackle the strategic work that drives success.

- **Promoting accountability that inspires peak performance without micromanaging:** You want your team to own their work—no hovering like a helicopter parent on the first day of school. Striking the right balance between support and autonomy not only boosts trust but also drives growth and ownership across the team.

- **Finding balance between your professional and personal life, so the lines don't blur to the point where you forget who you are outside of work:** It's easy to get sucked into the constant demands of work, but if you don't prioritize developing other parts of yourself, you'll suffer. Enter straightforward techniques to help you set boundaries and make time for the things that matter to you.

These are more than professional survival strategies; they're designed to help you level up as a person, because great leadership means you're staying true to who you are and growing both professionally and personally, leading with heart, authenticity, and the kind of integrity that inspires others to do the same (and maybe even getting a decent night's sleep).

No amount of commanding, micromanaging, or sending out a 12-page email can instantly enlist people's support or get them to buy in. Same with barking orders and hoping for compliance. The path we're walking is about inspiring, connecting, and building trust. It's more like trying to convince someone to join an important cause: if you're genuinely excited and show how it benefits them, people are more likely to jump on board.

Let me be clear: this book isn't a two-second cheat code. It's about committing to practice the fundamentals people actually care about at work. Once you've got them down, you'll have an edge.

Nope, leadership isn't neat and tidy. And, there's no perfect blueprint. But if you're ready to start leading with more intention, more focus, and more confidence, then let's dive in. You're already on your way to becoming the kind of leader who wants to have a bigger impact. All that's left is to take the first step.

Welcome to *Quick Leadership*. Let's do this together.

1 Be the Leader They Want to Work For

Let's face it: People aren't quitting jobs—they're quitting *bosses*. Workplace disillusionment is higher than ever, and "quiet quitting"? It isn't just a TikTok trend but a survival tactic. Being a leader worth sticking around for isn't optional, folks. It's your competitive edge.

But want to know something reassuring? The best leaders aren't bulletproof superheroes in capes. They're approachable. They're grounded. *They're human.* They set the tone for how work *feels*, not just how it gets done. They're willing to shield their teams from nonsense, amplify their people's wins, and create a space where showing up feels like an opportunity—not an obligation. (*Plus, come on, capes would totally get caught in those heavy office doors while you're trying to badge in with your ID.*) This chapter isn't about "management buzzwords" or performing leadership. It's about actionable, real-talk strategies that make you the kind of leader others willingly follow— even when things get tough. We'll cover everything from being the team's "sh!t umbrella" (yup, you read that right) to rethinking urgency culture and giving difficult feedback like a pro.

And I get it—personally. I've worked for toxic bosses who made me question my worth, I've managed teams, gotten promoted, and been laid off, and in my consultant roles I've assessed great workplaces to help them become even better, coaching leaders on embracing people-first leadership. Every insight I share comes from lived experience and a deep commitment to finding practical strategies that work. You're not alone in this journey. And I'm here to equip you with tools that can make a real difference. (And trust me, if I survived those kinds of bosses, you can too! I'm practically OSHA-certified in workplace chaos and re-orgs.)

Know this: You don't need a C-suite title to lead like this. You just need to decide you're done with outdated boss tropes and committed to be a leader people actually *want* to follow. Ready? Let's build something worth staying for.

Tip 1: Be the Sh!t Umbrella

Shield Your Team from the Storm

We've all been there: Work can be a circus of chaos—urgent-but-not-really deadlines, endless meetings that should've been emails, and last-minute "fire drills" that no one saw coming. Your team is in the thick of it, but that, my friend, is where you step in—not as a micromanager, but as the ultimate *sh!t umbrella*.

What's a sh!t umbrella, you ask? It's the leader who shields their team from workplace nonsense—unnecessary stress, fake emergencies, and random distractions—so the team can focus, thrive, and actually *enjoy* doing great work. Being this umbrella challenges you to manage upward, set boundaries, and sift through the demands that keep your team from shining. (And don't worry, this isn't shirking—it's just being the "do not disturb" setting they didn't know they had.)

A great illustration of this came from a leader I coached, Stefan. He managed a marketing team launching a big campaign. Just days before launch, an executive swooped in with "urgent" changes—wanting to rewrite key messaging and redo graphics last-minute. The worst part is that my client didn't even feel like the changes made sense! Instead of yanking his team into chaotic all-nighters, he calmly asked, "What's the larger goal of these changes?" and then "What's the consequence of staying the course?"" After some light discussion and awkward silences, the exec admitted the campaign was solid as-is. The team stayed on track, the launch went smoothly, and Stefan protected his people from unnecessary hits and burnout. *That's leadership.*

Filter the Faux-Urgency

You know the pattern: "We need this *ASAP!*" (Translation: "I just remembered this existed.") One of the most powerful things you can do as a leader is ask *why*. Try "Tell me more about the actual deadline," "Why is this urgent?" and "What happens if it's done next week instead of tomorrow?" Challenge false urgency before it hits your team's plates. Yes, if it's a real fire, rally the troops. If not, challenge ridiculous timelines, negotiate for more realistic ones, or take on the task yourself if it can't wait.

Kill the Chaos Meetings

You've seen 'em: meetings scheduled with zero context or 30 minutes' notice that somehow become *your* team's problem. Before you forward that invite to your team member like it's a hot potato, pause. Then try this: Get clarity before committing that you or your staff will attend. Ask, "Hey, what role do you need me/Sarabeth to play here?" or "What decisions need to be made?" Those who invited you might grumble at first, but they'll get used to you vetting attendance (and usually, respect you for it).

If it's just a status check or a meeting for the sake of meeting, skip it or ask for a quick update of minutes instead. Protect yours and your team's focus time—don't let it go to waste. And hey, sometimes being a little unconventional is exactly what's needed to protect their time. I still laugh thinking of my former manager who was working on setting more assertive boundaries for our team. He said he channeled his inner fierce bouncer at the most VIP club in order to do it. Ha! I liked to imagine him giving the "bouncer stare" to anything that didn't have a legit invite.

Provide Air Cover

The dreaded "Can you *just* ...?" requests are the silent assassins of productivity. Teach your team to recognize these quick hits and back your teammates up when they push back. If the request isn't a priority, encourage them to protect everyone's focus by tactfully saying something like "We're all hands on deck with [current project]. Can we revisit this late next week?"

Or, if someone tries to add extra tasks beyond the agreed scope, remind your team it's okay to set a boundary with a statement like "This wasn't part of the original plan, and adding it now will impact our budget/schedule/outputs. Let's discuss how we can fit this in once we've completed [priority task]." If, as a last resort, your team needs to send the request to you, let them know they can.

Have Their Backs—Loudly

When leadership starts piling on, step up as your team's advocate. Say, "We can take this on, but it'll push back these projects. How do you want to adjust the timeline?" Framing it this way not only shows you're solution-focused, but it also ensures your team's efforts get the recognition they deserve.

And when your team is killing it, don't keep it quiet—be their PR machine. Shine a spotlight on their wins and make sure everyone knows who's behind the success.

Let's not pretend: Being the sh!t umbrella isn't glamorous; in fact to be fair, the daily blocking and tackling can be exhausting. But for your people, it's game-changing. It's the shield they need from the stuff that doesn't matter so they can *crush* the stuff that does. When your people know you've got their backs, that you're willing to act, not just say words, they'll show up not just because they *have* to but because they *want* to. And that's how you lead a team that people never want to leave.

Ready to wield that umbrella like a pro? Let's go.

Tip 2: Open the Floor (Not Just Your Door)

I once coached a director-level client who was losing employees left and right. When I asked if she thought her team felt comfortable approaching her, she proudly said, "My door's always open." To that, I countered, "So what?"

She blinked, taken aback, shifting slightly in her seat. After a beat, she let out a nervous chuckle. "Well ... I mean, they *could* come to me."

Here's why it's not enough to say, "My door's always open." For a start, anyone can say that. Heck, even a vending machine could have an "open door." Second, just because there's an open door doesn't automatically mean your team feels safe or empowered to walk through it. Remember, employees are acutely aware of the power differential between you and them, so honest input won't just come on its own. You have to create an atmosphere where upward feedback is not just welcomed, but actively encouraged. Without that, the door ... well, it might as well be closed with a steel padlock!

It's About More Than Access

True approachability should feel like a real invitation, one that says, *I'm ready to listen, no judgment or defensiveness here* (and no rushing you out the door with my iced cappuccino in hand). So how do you make your office feel like a safe zone? A sanctuary where your team knows their voice matters?

Break the seal yourself. Regularly ask your team members what they think—*really think*—about things like project direction, team dynamics, a transition they've been making, and their workload. For example, you just announced a new directive to your team. You might say something afterward like "Okay, I'd like to hear from each of you about one concern you have and one opportunity you see with the new direction." Doing this regularly demonstrates that you want and need their input. Of course, just as important is *how* you receive their responses. People won't just wander into your office if they don't feel like their concerns will be heard with curiosity, respect, and attention. (*Basically, you're aiming for trusted-advice-giver energy, not "this better be good" gatekeeper.*)

Make Feedback Feel Safe, Not Scary

You know what's worse than not having an open door? Having a door that's always open but a boss who's always glancing at the clock, turning toward their screen or canceling check-ins like it's a sport. When someone finally speaks up, they get rushed through their thoughts like they're holding up the line at the deli.

The goal isn't just being accessible. It's making sure that when people *do* come to you, they feel heard, unrushed, and taken seriously. That kind of psychological safety doesn't appear overnight. It's built in the quiet, repeated moments when you stay present and listen all the way through.

Start small: regular check-ins, both formal and casual, where you actually have the time and attention to ask things like "What's working for you? What's not?" or "What could make things easier right now?" If an interruption bursts through, go out of your way to defer it until later. Because if every conversation feels like a speed round, don't be surprised when you only get surface-level stuff. Build in a beat. Sometimes the best feedback shows up in the final minutes, right when someone realizes you're actually sticking around to hear it.

Receive Feedback Without Ego

You want your team to be open with you? Then show them how. Lead by example. Be transparent about the feedback you receive and what you do with it. Perhaps you and your team are discussing ideas for how to improve ongoing communication. If you get upward feedback that says, "Hey, I think you could set clearer expectations at the start of meetings. People seem confused about what they're supposed to weigh in on," you could respond with something like "That's a great point. Next week, I'll try kicking things off with a quick 'Here's what we're deciding today' so we stay on track. Let's see how it goes.'"

And if you're caught off guard by some input, my go-to response in that situation is "Thanks for sharing that. Let me take a day to reflect on it, and I'll get back to you with what I'll do differently next time." When you show that you're taking others' feedback seriously, your team will be more likely to speak up in the future.

And remember, feedback runs both ways. Encourage your team to hold one another accountable too. Peer feedback can often be more immediate and impactful than top-down suggestions. For example, once a team member shares their approach for an upcoming presentation, prompt the other members to offer constructive suggestions or additions. It builds a culture where everyone is invested in mutual success and continuous improvement.

So do more than open the door. Bake probing questions (looking at the positive and negative) into your meeting designs, invite peer feedback, and model that you yourself are receptive to others' views. Start there, and the conversations will follow.

Tip 3: Humanize the Hard Stuff

Leadership is being an unshakable mountain, immune to doubt and criticism, with a halo glowing above your head, making flawless decisions in your sleep. Ha! If you believe that, we've got an Everest-sized problem. No, the best leaders aren't perfection or omniscience in SVP form—they're human. And that same latitude they give themselves to be real and fallible gives others permission to be human.

Research backs this up. One study by Dr. Jasmine Hu and colleagues at the Ohio State University found that when people have a humble leader who acknowledges their own limitations and mistakes, team members are more likely to share their knowledge, voice their concerns, and engage in improvement-oriented behaviors.[1] Sounds like a pretty welcome ripple effect, doesn't it?

If your memory is a highlight reel of awkward leadership moments, good—you're halfway there. But it's okay too if you don't know where to start in terms of mining your own mistakes. You can consider these examples of mistakes that are the most common ones I hear as a coach—shown by category. Like any good misstep, they make ideal teachable moments:

- **Collaboration:** Misaligned goals, poor communication *(You dropped the ball on sharing updates or assumed everyone was on the same page.)*
- **Relational:** Lack of empathy, conflict avoidance *(You steamrolled someone's concern or ghosted a tough conversation.)*
- **Decision-making:** Analysis paralysis, risk aversion *(You sat on a choice so long the window closed, so someone else made it for you.)*
- **Leadership:** Micromanagement, lack of recognition *(You hovered like a drone or forgot to shout someone out for great work.)*
- **Customer/client:** Overpromising, ignoring feedback *(You said yes to keep the peace ... then scrambled to deliver—or didn't.)*

Own Your Mistakes and Share What You've Learned

I get it—nobody likes being wrong. Just ask my husband what kind of dinner table debater I am. But here's the truth: When you as a leader own your mistakes, you communicate to your team: "We don't have to pretend to be perfect to do great work." You're not *acting* vulnerable (when it's not genuine) for sympathy or martyrdom. It's about showing your team that vulnerability isn't the liability they worry it is, but a strength that facilitates openness and growth. That could mean you feel uncertain and name it aloud, or that you're being emotionally honest with your colleagues about something uncomfortable or new for you. You're choosing sincerity, candor, and realness over your ego.

I remember one presentation I was giving to a pharmaceutical company, where I asked the president ahead of time how I could tailor my material for the audience. His response really struck me: "Two things I hope you'll hit home: truth and courage. We had a major drug fail recently, and I'm convinced it's because I created a culture where people didn't feel they could air their concerns."

I've never forgotten that moment because of how much ownership he took. He wasn't blaming his team or the regulators or external circumstances. He was standing up and saying, "This is on me," and acknowledging how the culture he built—or didn't build—impacted the outcome. *That's leadership at its best.* By taking responsibility for a dysfunction in the culture, he not only showed integrity, but he also set a powerful example for his team: *I didn't get it right—and I see how that shaped where we are. Let's use that so we can move forward.*

Why Vulnerability Builds Trust

When leaders are open about mistakes, it unclenches the whole team. No more hiding errors like you're smuggling snacks into a movie theater. If your team sees you as someone who can admit when you're wrong—without a wall of defensiveness—they'll feel safer doing the same. What's especially cool is that this creates a more innovative, communicative, and resilient team. People aren't afraid to raise concerns or admit when they're struggling. Instead of hiding problems, they air and tackle 'em head-on.

So next time you make a mistake—whether it's a process breakdown, a missed deadline, or a miscommunication—don't sweep it under the rug or deflect blame. Stand up, own it, and share what you've learned. It can be as sweet and simple as "I think I made a mistake on this," or "I think I was wrong about that earlier." Then encourage your team to do the same. Create an environment where it's okay to be imperfect, because in doing so, you're telling your team: *Nobody's flawless, and nobody needs to pretend to be.*

Tip 4: Rethink Urgency Culture

Let's start with the obvious truth: Urgency isn't some virtue. Too much of it destroys people's focus, not to mention their equilibrium and well-being. And yet the "need it five minutes ago" mentality dominates so many workplaces, turning a task into an emergency and deadlines into a game of constant whack-a-mole. And sometimes leaders don't even notice they're just going along with it—not even questioning why things need to be done yesterday!

Since when did we decide that no one should ever have to wait for anything?!

As a young management consultant at a fancy firm, this thinking was so culturally normal, so ingrained in us, that we'd treat every client request like a leak in a boat; if we didn't attend to it ASAP, we'd surely sink. Cortisol spikes were practically built into the job description. If a client asked to change the font color on a slide, we'd drop everything because, clearly, *Arial Blue* was a matter of corporate survival. If they wanted a data point rechecked (even one we'd triple-verified), we'd scramble to rerun the numbers *immediately*, just in case. The urgency was often artificial, but the stress? Very real.

The result of an "urgency culture" isn't productivity; it's burnout. Employees aren't more effective when they're in a perpetual rush. They're stressed, drained, and distracted. And you, as a leader, are part of that equation. You might be unconsciously reinforcing the very thing that makes your team feel like they're on a 70-mile-per-hour hamster wheel: always spinning but never getting anywhere. Or you can be a different kind of pacesetter.

What "Urgency Culture" Does to Your Team

When urgency becomes the default setting, it tricks people into believing they should be constantly sprinting, never slowing down to think. That can hurt decision-making—prioritizing speed rather than substance—and make people hesitate to admit mistakes, ask questions, or challenge ideas for fear they'll be seen as "slowing down the process." Here, creativity takes a backseat to quick fixes. And innovation? Forget about it.

It can even cause adverse health effects over time. In the *Harvard Business Review* article "The Insidious Effects of Hurrying," burnout expert and author Kandi Wiens writes:

> This relentless urgency can result in a phenomenon known as "hurry sickness," a term first introduced in 1974 by cardiologists Meyer Friedman and R.H. Rosenman to describe the damaging effects of Type A (i.e., high-achieving) behavior on cardiovascular health. Hurry sickness isn't a diagnosable condition, but it encapsulates a set of behaviors and emotions—impatience, chronic rushing, and a constant sense of time scarcity—that can wreak havoc on a person's physical and mental well-being.[2]

The Solution: Prioritize with Intention

It's time to turn the dial from "urgency culture" to a more intentional, grounded, and care-driven approach. You do not need to respond to every email in an hour or race to meet an unrealistic deadline. It's about lining up your team's efforts with meaningful priorities and creating the space for thoughtful decision-making. If you want to stand up to urgency culture, take it step by step, using these guideposts:

- **Step 1: Set clear priorities.** As a leader, part of your job is to sift through the noise and help your team focus. This means clearly defining what matters most and what can wait—*you're the sh!t umbrella, remember!?* Instead of cramming everything into one week or day, take a step back and assess your team's workload. Think: "Here's what matters most today, and here's why. Let's focus on this first, then we'll tackle the rest."

- **Step 2: Give your team time to breathe.** Once priorities are clear, normalize a workflow that allows your team time to work at a sustainable pace. Encourage breaks, manageable workloads, and flexible deadlines (where appropriate). Urgency culture breeds a sense of scarcity and exhaustion but you're replacing that with *sustainable work over time*. Think: "The work will still get done. Let's just do it in a way that doesn't leave us all feeling like wet noodles by Friday."

- **Step 3: Model the behavior you want to see.** As with everything in leadership, it starts with you. If you're setting a standard of rushed work and constant pressure, your team will follow suit. But if you take the time to pause, reflect, and say "Enough" at times, your team will feel empowered to do the same. Think: "If I'm constantly scrambling, they'll think that's the only way to work. I need to show them there's value in thinking things through before diving in."

The Power of Protecting Your People

Wanna make work a place where people feel seen, heard, and valued? Stop rewarding hustle at the expense of well-being. Communicate to your people that it's okay to take the time necessary to do the job right. That'll encourage them to view their work as something worth putting thought and care into, rather than something to hurry up and check off the list.

So the next time you feel questionably rushed, ask yourself: *Is this the most important thing right now, or are we just moving quickly for the sake of it?*

Tip 5: Signal Belonging

Do you actively cultivate belonging? The kind where people feel like they're truly part of something important—like their experience is valued, their contributions count, and their voices matter? (Notice we're not talking about token gestures or repeating empty platitudes about inclusion.)

If you miss the mark on making belonging part of your culture, you risk disillusionment, apathy, and that awful sense that there are insiders and outsiders. But nail this, and you'll create a team that's motivated, engaged, and loyal. Here's how you do it.

Give Meaningful Intros

How you introduce people is not a trivial thing! In fact, it can make all the difference in integrating a person into your team and helping them start with momentum and credibility on their side. Instead of the breezy and vague "Here's Sarah, who'll be working with us on IT," try "This is Sarah, who'll be our director of IT—she's the engine behind the new features in our website and app and we're excited to have her expertise in A, B and C." Another example might be "Please meet [Name], who's not only our [title], but also especially talented at [skill or trait, e.g., creativity, leadership, problem-solving]. They're a big reason our team has been able to [specific success]." When you boost someone's status by highlighting their unique contributions, expertise, or qualities, you emphasize their value to the group. And you're telling your team, "Hey, I see you and you matter here." Simple but effective.

Don't Hoard Credit Like It's Your Last Cookie

I'll never forget working days, nights, and weekends on a tedious Excel project as a young consultant—only to have my boss stand up and present it at an offsite, saying things like "I led the entire effort by ... ," "I figured out the best way to ... ," and "I tackled the challenge by ..." Ugh! Hearing her continually say "I" effectively covered me in an invisibility cloak, and it stung. There's nothing more demoralizing than doing great work and having it go unnoticed.

So when someone on your team crushes it, shine the spotlight on them. Don't just throw them a generic "good job" and move on. Recognize the details that made their contribution stand out. Say something like "I want to shout out Leo for totally elevating that design project. It was his idea to do X that took it to the next level, and we wouldn't have landed that client without it," or "I know this was a particularly tedious task, Deena, but your commitment to quality is noticed and appreciated." When people feel like their hard work is seen and appreciated, they're more likely to stick around and keep delivering (a clear upgrade from rage-applying to jobs at 2 a.m. with a pint of ice cream in hand).

Yield the Floor

Yes, you're the leader, but sometimes stepping back is the best move. Defer to others when it's their area of knowledge or expertise.

This is less about giving up control, and more about recognizing that the best outcomes spring when everyone's strengths are valued and used. If your marketing lead is the expert on customer data, don't step in by default. Instead say, "This is your area of strength, [Name], so I'll leave it to you to guide us," or "I'll defer to you on this, [Name], you know it best." When you yield and put the mic in someone else's hand, you help them grow in confidence and ownership of their work. It's a win-win that fosters a more collaborative, belonging-oriented team dynamic.

Respect Different Workstyles

Here's another way to stoke belonging. While working at Deloitte, I got to consult to their "crown jewel" clients on their teams' strengths and the composition of their different workstyles. So while I might've discovered a diverse team at a bank that was heavier in logical, analytical driver types, another team I'd work with at an ad agency may be composed of more big-picture thinkers and future-oriented folks.

My big takeaway from advising dozens of teams at the world's most innovative companies? That *difference* in workstyle that annoys you about your teammate or boss is very likely a hidden superpower for your team. Whether it's someone's tendency to dive into the details when you prefer to focus on the big picture, or a colleague's cautious decision-making style when you lean toward taking risks, those collective differences are actually the ingredients for a stronger team. When you don't challenge your own disdain for people who work differently than you, you miss the chance to see how that contrast can actually be your team's secret weapon. Like how Sarah's meticulous tracking keeps big ideas from floating into the ether—and how Mark's bold pitches push the team beyond Status Quo City.

Belonging Is an Invitation You Extend Every Day

Creating a culture of belonging is something you actively choose to do every day. It's in the words you use and the small actions. It's a gentle prompt, like "What do you think about this, Maria?" When you make people feel like they belong, as full card-carrying members of the team, you create a space where they can flourish. I'll dive deeper into these topics in Chapter 8, The Inclusion Power Moves That Matter, where we'll explore more strategies to help you elevate others. Remember, belonging isn't some bonus; it's the baseline.

Tip 6: Hold Your Horses (and Your Hot Takes)

You know the feeling: Someone presents an idea, and your brain is already two steps ahead—thinking of ways to solve it, fix it, implement it, or improve it. But before you race to be the first one to speak, try this: Hit pause rather than hitting the gas. Give a person space to voice their thoughts fully. Some pretty cool magic happens when you wait a beat and give things air. It's like people hear you saying, "I'm not the only expert here—and the more we tap into our collective wisdom, the stronger we get." Then a real conversation can unfold.

Don't Rush In—Let Them Speak First

As a leader, your insights are valuable—but so are everyone else's. Let your team speak first, and you're showing them that you value their perspective, even when it's different from yours. So how can you put this into practice? Try giving yourself a substitute for speaking. I've coached leaders to make a bodily movement if they need to—to replace speaking up with "the answer." They can make a body shift in their chair, simply take a swallow, or even take a nice deep breath, expanding their chest, to allow for that cushion of silence. That's where the blank canvas for your team lies. Let them talk before you hand down conclusions, and watch your team's trust and ideas blossom.

Oh, and here's an important signal to look for. If there's a silence in your meetings and everyone then looks to you, it might mean that your team is used to you jumping in. This is a great opportunity to invite others to speak instead. If they always default to you to start speaking, well, now you have your action item! So sit in that quiet for a moment—looking at them with anticipatory interest—and they'll start to speak.

Let the Ideas Breathe

Giving people's inputs some oxygen creates the space and freedom for ideas to develop and evolve. And part of that is embracing the early, messy phase of ideation. So instead of seeking out polished proposals, you're encouraging even half-formed thoughts. This often leads to unexpected, innovative insights. Example prompts might include "This doesn't need to be fully fleshed out—what's your initial thought?" "Let's hear the rough version first—we can refine it together," or "How might that look in practice, even if the details aren't clear yet?" In short, "Let the Ideas Breathe" is about resisting the impulse to judge or resolve too quickly. It's allowing space for collective thought to unfold naturally. That right there is what makes collaboration more fun, dynamic, and innovative.

The Art of Really Listening

The next time you feel the urge to speak, pause for just a moment longer than usual. Don't just hear the words—*listen*. This is the same technique my kids learned in the third grade. It's called *whole body listening*. If a kid is technically listening with their ears but their back is facing the teacher, and their right hand is fidgeting with their sneaker laces while their left hand is fishing around in their desk, then they're not *really listening*, are they? The same goes for adults. That means your ears are intently perked up but your body is also in alignment.

You're squarely facing the person speaking, and you have an engaged, encouraging, and expectant look on your face. This communicates "I'm here, I'm following, and I value what you're saying."

Ask Provocative Questions, Not Just for Quick Fixes

Great leaders know that the right question can spark powerful conversations and lead to breakthrough thinking. Rather than just jumping in with your own solution or feedback, you can also try asking questions that challenge your team's thinking. For example, "How would you approach this if there were no limitations or constraints?" or "What's the one thing we haven't considered yet?" These questions shift the focus from you to them. Let your team wrestle with their ideas and discover solutions you might never have anticipated.

Quiet Leadership Is the Real Power Move

As a leader, you don't have to fill every silence. Sometimes doing less is actually doing more. When you resist the urge to always step in with your thoughts, you're multiplying the moments your team can shine. Let them lead and be prepared to be amazed.

Tip 7: Skip "Do You Have a Minute?"

You know when you're deep in work mode, fully focused and in the flow, and then … knock knock. "Hey, got a minute?" *Poof. There goes your genius, mid-sentence—it packed its bags and left the building.* Multiply that practice by a few times a week, expanded to your whole team, and you've got a recipe for frustration and lost productivity.

For leaders, the "Do you have a minute?" approach feels efficient. It's quick, casual, and gets your question answered. But for *your team?* It's disruptive. It's stress-inducing. And it signals that your time is more valuable than theirs. Contrary to what your calendar might suggest, it's not. Besides, has anyone ever met a "just a minute" request that *actually* takes only one minute!?

Respect the Mental Bandwidth Bank

Think of your team's mental energy like a bank account. Focus-intensive tasks—like writing reports, crafting strategies, or coding—require hefty withdrawals. Every unexpected interruption is a surprise fee they didn't authorize.

When you pop in unannounced, you're essentially saying, "My immediate need trumps whatever you're working on." It's not intentional, but it's the message received. Respecting someone's mental bandwidth means recognizing that uninterrupted time is sacred in today's distraction-packed world.

But What If It's Urgent?

Of course, emergencies happen. True urgency—think system outages or client crises—warrants immediate action. But you know as well as I do that most "urgent" issues are just things we'd prefer to resolve right now. A recent study in the journal *Work & Stress* actually showed that interruptions from bosses take up more time compared to interruptions from colleagues, and—wait for it—employees feel a stronger need to respond to interruptions from their supervisors.[3] So before you interrupt, ask yourself:

- Can this wait until our next scheduled check-in?
- Could I send a quick message summarizing the issue and asking when they're free?

That little, momentary pause can prevent unnecessary disruptions while keeping things moving.

How to Break the Habit (Without Feeling Disconnected)

Just because you're popping in unannounced less often means you can't stay synced with people. Try these alternatives for connecting with your people purposefully:

- **Schedule office hours.** Set designated times for open-door chats. Communicate this clearly: "Need to bounce an idea off me? My office hours are Tuesdays, 2–4 p.m."

- **Use a shared calendar.** Encourage team members to block focus time on their calendars, and do the same yourself. This visual reminder makes it clear when someone is heads-down and when they're open for collaboration.

- **Embrace asynchronous updates.** Not everything requires a real-time conversation. Use project management tools or shared docs for updates and questions that can be handled without interrupting someone's workflow.

Be the Leader Who Gets It

Leaders who respect their team's time earn loyalty and trust. Skipping "Do you have a minute?" shows you value their focus, not just their availability. It also makes your team more likely to want to come together when it truly matters.

So before popping in with a quick question, take a breath and consider your team's time (and maybe ask yourself if it's Slack-able, schedulable, or just unnecessary). You're modeling a culture of mutual respect. And your team's productivity (and sanity) will thank you.

Tip 8: Praise Publicly, Coach Privately

People are starved for recognition. In fact, nearly 80% of employees feel they'd be more productive if they were recognized *more frequently*.

Talk about a hunger pang! The thing about acknowledging wins—particularly in an open, public way—is that it creates what I call a "triple ripple" effect: The person being praised feels valued, their peers see what success looks like, and the team's morale lifts. *That's* what I call a leadership power move.

Imagine an ordinary team meeting where you shout out someone's brilliant client presentation, something you know they prepared for thoughtfully. Suddenly, the vibe shifts—the person's effort feels worthwhile, others are motivated to step up—the acknowledgment creates buzz.

The best bosses do this in a way that's specific. Skip vague platitudes like "Great job!" and try "You handled that tough client call with such grace. Even when it would've been easy to overpromise, you kept the project in scope. Well done!" Precision and authenticity in what you share shows you're paying attention. Plus, it gives them a clear template to use for future behavior you want to see more of!

Make Coaching a Private Affair

Feedback usually stings the most in front of an audience. When you critique someone publicly, you risk embarrassing them, damaging trust, and creating a culture of fear. No one does their best work while bracing to get publicly body-slammed. Now let's apply this to a common-enough situation. Imagine that a team member mishandles a meeting. If you correct them on the spot in front of their peers, they'll likely feel self-conscious and shut down. But if you pull them aside after and say, "Let's talk about how to steer conversations when things go off track," they're more likely to listen, learn, and improve.

Now as much as I love a good BLT or my hometown Philly cheesesteak—and I really love them—I have to caution you against using the "feedback sandwich" (good feedback, followed by bad, followed by good). It can feel forced. Instead, be straightforward yet compassionate: "Your presentation had great insights. Let's work on tightening the data points next time so your message lands even stronger."

Balance Recognition and Reality

Be intentional about both praise and coaching. Overpraise can dilute sincerity, while too much critique can deflate spirits. Strike a balance: Shout out wins regularly, but coach behind closed doors when improvement is needed.

How do you put this into action?

1. **Create a praise ritual.** Start meetings with a "Win of the Week" or "Shoutout Spotlight" to celebrate success stories. It's fast, energizing, and team-building. And you share the load of calling out good work; it doesn't have to come only from you.

2. **Develop a coaching habit.** Schedule monthly one-on-ones focused on growth, with no agenda other than development. Think, "Let's workshop the core business development techniques that make the biggest difference."

3. **Be consistent.** Praise shouldn't happen only when the whim strikes. Beyond building recognition into your agenda, give yourself a shorthand for recognition that makes it easy to initiate. You don't need 43 lines to memorize, but even two or three sentence starters you regularly reach for like—"I noticed how you ... ," "I appreciate that you ... ," or "I'm impressed that you ..."—make it part of your natural day-to-day language.

There's a Time and a Place

When people trust that you'll celebrate them openly but correct them privately, it promotes an essential kind of security. No more flinching, second-guessing, or playing small—they're free to do their best work. Public praise fuels motivation. Private coaching fosters growth. Do both consistently, and you'll be the kind of leader people trust, respect, and choose to follow—even when times get tough.

Tip 9: Ditch the Boss Image: Embrace the Leader Persona

Let's play a little matching game:

Management is about tasks.

Leading and mentoring is about people.

Now look back at your last few workdays. For each significant interaction you had, would you categorize your primary focus as *management* (tasks) or *leading and mentoring* (people)? What's your current ratio? Where would you *like* that ratio to be?

If you want to lead a team that sticks around, stops dreading Monday mornings, and actually cares about their work, you need to make the conscious shift from managing projects to mentoring people. And let me say, having coached many a leader, that change is entirely within your reach.

Managing Is Bare Minimum Behavior—Start Mentoring

Think about it like this: Managing is transactional. It calls for checklists, deadlines, and updates—essential, sure, but uninspiring. Anyone can manage a to-do list, but not everyone can inspire people to *want* to crush it.

Imagine being known as "the manager who tracks deliverables" versus "the leader who builds careers." Which legacy sounds better?

Be the Career Catalyst

Think back to the best leader you ever had. Chances are, they didn't just assign tasks. They challenged you, believed in you, and opened doors. They were career catalysts.

I can still remember my mentor, Jane, suggesting the unthinkable when I was 24: "Why don't *you* give the client presentation?" It felt like a huge leap, but her faith in me sparked something I didn't know I had. I took her up on it, and it gave me a boost of self-belief I've carried ever since. Be that leader. Swap "How are we going to get ready for next week's presentation?" for "What are some skills you want to grow when it comes to client presentations? Let's see if there's a chance to put them into practice next week."

You can make this an even more regular topic of conversation by implementing "Grow and Go" check-ins. Every few months, ask your team two things: "What's one thing you want to *grow* in your role?" and "What's one thing you want to *go* after next?" Then help them map a path.

Oh, and if you really connect with this topic, sit tight: I have more on this in Chapter 4, Tip 2.

Feedback That Feeds Growth

Just like we've explored in other tips, good feedback is specific feedback. Make a point to offer precise input, then check your tone. Is it fueling them or flattening them? Here's an example to show you the difference.

- *Bad feedback:* "You missed the mark on that client presentation."
- *Mentor-style feedback:* "Your presentation showed tons of depth, but next time, let's tighten the key points to make the message land faster."

See the difference? One demoralizes; the other energizes.

Lead Like the Mentor You Wish You Had

Mentors lead by example. If you're asking your team to innovate, take risks, or level up, show them how it's done.

Share your own learning curve stories. Admit when you're still figuring things out. Leaders who say, "I'm working on that skill, too," create a culture of continuous improvement. It's not weakness—it's relatability.

For example, here's a personal story I like to share with my mentees. I once submitted an audition video to teach an online course and received brutally honest feedback from not two or three but seven producers. Reading the page-long list of bulleted feedback I felt like I'd been punched in the gut, about as vulnerable and exposed as a person standing naked in Times Square. But you know what? The producers were right. I took their suggestions to heart, and not only did it land me the gig, but it also set me on a path where I spend a significant part of my career in front of the camera—and today I actually enjoy it.

So share your "gut-punch" moments and what you learned. It can help someone else learn a lesson quicker, show them they're not alone, and humanize you and build trust.

Mentorship Wins Loyalty

People don't usually quit jobs where they feel seen, heard, and developed. They quit managers and environments that underinvest in them.

When you become a mentor-leader, you're creating a movement of leaders who'll develop other leaders. The cascade keeps going. And you're someone they'll remember long after they've outgrown their roles.

So, manage less. Mentor more. Your ultimate contribution as a leader won't be the answers you provided, but the capabilities you nurtured in others.

2 Cultivating an Intentional Team Culture

Culture is the force—both visible and invisible—that shapes how work feels, day in and day out. It's how people feel after back-to-back meetings, how conflicts are resolved (or avoided), and even the degree of comfort people feel asking for help without worrying it'll be seen as incompetence. It's the difference between coming home with energy to be present or dragging the weight of unresolved stress into your evenings. It's what makes Sunday nights feel like a fresh start, instead of a countdown of palpitations to another week of dread.

The truth? Culture happens whether or not you're intentional about it. And when you leave it to chance, dysfunction and disengagement can creep in like weeds through sidewalk cracks (and boy, are those weeds resilient!).

A lot of people mistake culture for their best-made plans. But it's much more that—culture is also what you abide and tolerate. The behavior, values, and standards within an organization are defined by what people allow to happen *without challenge*. That's true whether there's a pervasive culture of fear, competition, trust, or collaboration. When negative behaviors or norms go unchecked, they become the unspoken rules of the workplace. On the flip side, consistently reinforcing positive values, rewarding people for them and holding people accountable, creates a culture where respect, integrity, and support thrive—even on the tough days.

In this chapter, we'll explore practical, fresh strategies to build a team vibe that hums with trust, mutual respect, and authentic positivity. I'm challenging you to embrace quirks (yes, even Dave's obsession with color-coded spreadsheets), celebrate wins (big, small, and "We survived that two-and-a-half-hour planning meeting!"), and confront challenges with curiosity, not blame. You'll learn how to design meetings that people actually *choose* to attend and create an environment where every team member feels empowered to contribute, innovate, and thrive. Importantly, you'll start setting the tone for well-being, not just talking about it.

Ready to ditch the stale team-building clichés (looking at you, trust falls) and craft a culture people can't stop raving about? Let's get to work.

Tip 1: Lead by Example: Wellness Starts with You

You don't just influence culture—you embody it. If you're constantly grinding, like sending emails at 2 a.m., don't be surprised when your team follows suit. I once worked for a boss who proudly mentioned how much unused vacation he had at the end of every year. I took that as a cue to skip my own time off, until I realized how totally out of sync that was with *my* human rhythms! On the flip side, if you model balance—working hard but also stepping away to refresh—your team will start to see wellness as a nonnegotiable part of success. That doesn't mean rigidly clocking out at the same exact time every day, but showing that excellence and taking care of yourself can coexist.

Take a Break, Make a Difference

We live in a world where it feels like we're supposed to be available 24/7. But consider this: You *get to* decide when and where to set limits. No one—not even your BFF—can do that for you. That might mean implementing breaks day to day or strategizing from a weekly lens how you'll build in recharging time. And, it can mean looking further afield at your month or year to consider how you're doing, what you want and need, and where planned breaks make sense. The point is respite and recharging are on your mind and you're actively factoring them into your life.

So rest by example. Show your team that leadership includes taking time off, stepping away for mental health breaks, and setting personal boundaries. You're saying, "I don't need to burn out to prove I'm committed—and neither do you." Boom. Powerful!

Tune into Rhythms and Cues

Intellectually, we know people aren't production machines—each operates with their own work rhythms, energy levels, and fluctuating needs. And yet "just power through it" still gets handed out like a cough drop for pneumonia. If your team is burned out after a series of intense deadlines or seems disengaged in meetings, these are signs that their energy is low. Ignoring these cues and pushing through isn't leadership. It's not admirable dedication either. It's burnout waiting to happen. Be the leader who notices and cares. Give your team permission to take a breather. Encourage flexible hours, mental health days, or a midafternoon reset. Your team's energy is finite, and it's your job to protect it.

Here are a few examples of ways to show you actually care:

- "I know it's been a tough stretch with deadlines, and I see how hard everyone's been working. I'm going to take a break [at this date/time]. If you need a break, feel free to take one."
- "It's been a busy few weeks, and I really appreciate everyone's dedication. Take some time to recharge if you need it. Your well-being comes first."
- "I've noticed the long hours you've been putting in, and I want to make sure you're not burning out. Take the time to reset if you need it."

- "You've been pushing hard lately, and I want to remind you that it's okay to take a break. Let's stay sharp by taking care of ourselves."

These messages and gestures demonstrate that you understand your people's energy isn't an infinite resource. Give them the license to recharge without guilt.

No More "Always-On" Culture

Retiring the "always-on" culture can start with you. Being constantly available doesn't mean you're a better leader anyway. It means you're setting unrealistic and unsustainable standards. So let go of the idea that "real leaders" never stop working. Whether on a day off, when your head should be hitting the pillow, or on your tropical vacation, the only "deliverable" should be a rested (and maybe slightly sunburnt) you.

As for how you can model "appropriately off" culture, consider making a fierce commitment not to respond to emails, Slacks, or texts after work hours. If you must, respond by saying "I'll get back to you tomorrow during work hours." When you have check-ins with your direct reports, share when you'll take time off, then ask when they plan to. If they don't have a plan, it's a great time to encourage them to make one. And model stepping away from your desk from time to time notification-free and letting your team know, "I'm stepping outside for a quick walk." These simple practices have the cumulative effect of creating a culture where breaks, rest, and boundaries are as normal as saying good morning.

Wellness Breaks = Team Breakthroughs

Remember, it's easy to become out of touch with how healthy your practices actually are. One American Psychological Association study found that 49% of those working in healthy workplaces—and 77% of those working in toxic workplaces—think their employer believes the workplace is healthier than it actually is.[1] It's a gap many leaders don't realize exists. The view on workplace well-being is often rosier at the top than it is on the ground.

That's why wellness breaks aren't a luxury; they're essential. A well-rested, mentally sharp team is more engaged and productive. And they're that much closer to tapping their creativity, collaboration, and highest-quality work. That's the power of a culture that values well-being: It shows in the way people connect, the energy in the room, and the quality of the work.

Tip 2: Recognize Burnout Red Flags

It's not just about the eyebags you show up with one day after a late night. Burnout happens like a slow leak in a tire. At first, you can barely feel it—something might feel only microscopically imbalanced. But if the signs pile up and you ignore them, you'll soon find yourself stuck on the side of the road, desperate and waiting for someone to come save you. *Ack!* Let's look closer at those subtle signs of burnout so we can stop them before they become full-blown exhaustion.

Fatigue: The Zombie Mode Syndrome

Maybe you've been there. Too much pushing it here, extending it there, and generally stretching your limits. That could be from overintensity, overwork, overstimulation, or good ol' overcommitting. So often we ask our teams to do these things (maybe not always directly) without noticing how cumulative the load has become.

When your team starts dragging through the day like extras from a zombie apocalypse, it's time to pay attention. You might notice them zoning out in meetings or looking lackluster and "gray." They probably also avoid contributing as much as usual and may struggle to look fully awake—even without a triple-shot espresso in hand.

- **Address It: Recharge, Don't Scold**

⇒ When fatigue sets in, resist the urge to say, "We're *all* tired!" and move on. That's not leadership—it's dismissal. Instead, say "I hear you. I see the team is looking pretty de-energized. Let's talk about what we can shift or pause to make this more sustainable." Then reassess workloads by delaying or parking-lotting certain projects and redistributing priorities.

Irritability: The Short Fuse Indicator

Like anyone who's ever tried to open those military-grade, double-walled, child-proof, NASA-engineered, seemingly welded-shut clamshell plastic packages knows—when stress builds, patience shrinks. That same barely contained frustration is what you might be seeing manifest as irritability within your team when they're burning out. That's when snarky comments, eye-rolls, and terse emails pop up. These are the moments when "Can't you just …" is dripping with annoyance, "Did you even read my email?" comes off curtly, and "Whatever" is whispered with a rumble of frustration.

Irritability is a major burnout warning sign, and it spreads like wildfire. A team member snapping at a colleague might be waving a red flag that something's wrong—not just someone having a "bad day."

- **Address It: Unload the Pressure Cooker**

⇒ Instead of reprimanding someone for their short fuse, open the door for honest conversations. Create a culture where some healthy venting, asking for help, or simply acknowledging tough times is okay. This might sound like "Hey, you seem a little stressed, is everything all right?"

"It sounds like you're dealing with a lot, how can I support you?" or even a simple "Rough day?" Empathy can defuse tension faster than a stern email ever could.

Disengagement: When They Check Out Without Leaving

Disengagement is the sneaky one. The employee who used to give 110% now barely manages 60%. They stop showing up to meetings on time, miss deadlines, and seem indifferent. Even the volunteer work they used to enjoy doing for an employee resource group seems a drag. This is often the first sign that burnout is quietly settling in, even before more obvious signs appear.

- **Address It: Reconnect, Don't Pressure**
⇒ Don't assume they've checked out for good. Schedule a one-on-one to ask how they're doing—no agenda, just genuine curiosity. You might say something like, "Hey, I've noticed you haven't seemed quite yourself lately, and I wanted to check in. How are things going?" or "Is there anything on your plate that's been weighing on you? I'm here to help." This is particularly important because employees often hesitate to voice concerns; a Microsoft study revealed that only 13.6% of employees indicate they raised concerns with their manager when it came to everyday workplace topics.[2] Maybe they're overwhelmed by personal issues or struggling with an unmanageable workload. Showing that you care about more than just their output can reignite their drive. Sometimes knowing someone is in their corner makes all the difference.

Prevent the Burnout Crash Before It Happens

Burnout's preventable, not inevitable. Stay vigilant for fatigue, irritability, and disengagement, so you can catch the signs early and intervene. Be willing to reassess those workloads, and to reevaluate priorities. Make sure your team has the support, resources, and time they need to recharge. A thriving team is a healthy team— make it your top priority.

Tip 3: Hold Regular Fish-Slappings

Between you and me, every team has a few stinky fish lying around. These are the issues everyone knows about but no one dares to address because they're awkward, uncomfortable, or just plain unpleasant. But when you ignore them, they fester like that forgotten stink in the fridge. That can leave people with resentment, disengagement, and just a seriously bad vibe.

What's a leader to do? *Create space for a "fish-slapping"*: that bold, slightly ridiculous meeting where everyone can slap their stinky fish onto the table and air the problems that are riling them. Plus, calling them "fish-slappings" brings some levity to the situation, which diffuses tension. (Hey, it's way better than calling them "the festering wounds of team dysfunction," right?) Normalizing these in your team's culture builds expectations and camaraderie around issues that could exacerbate but don't have to—and shouldn't. Think of it as opening the windows and letting the stale air out before it turns toxic.

I can remember the first fish-slapping meeting I attended. My unit leader called everyone in and over the subsequent hours we talked one by one about the simmering issues: unclear roles and responsibilities, the frustration of changing mandates from leadership, and perceptions of less-than-great communication about a new realignment. It was awkward at first, like we were all trying to tiptoe around the mess. But by the end we'd at least gotten everything out in the open. Not all the issues were solved right then, but it did give us a clearer path forward and made it a lot easier to tackle them head-on together. It also made it normal to talk about cringy stuff.

The Power of the Fish-Slap

The beauty of a fish-slapping is that it allows your team to voice their concerns without fear of judgment or backlash. It's not Blameville, it's a place to productively clear the air and solve the problem before it becomes a full-blown culture killer.

Ground Rules for a Successful Fish-Slap

Don't worry, this isn't a free-for-all gripe fest. You can create a positive, constructive climate with these simple ground rules:

- **No blame, no shame:** No witch hunts. Keep it constructive and focused on problem-solving, not finger-pointing.

- **Be specific:** General comments like "The feel of the team is off" don't help anyone. Get into specifics: "I'm frustrated by constant last-minute changes to deadlines." You can even get specific, anonymous input on "stinky fish" through a quick pre-fish-slapping survey. That way, you hear from people ahead of time who might be less comfortable speaking up at the real thing.

- **Solutions over complaints:** Encourage your team to propose possible solutions, or at least suggestions for how things could improve. A fish-slap meeting isn't a pity party; it's a dialogue and solutioning session.

How to Run a Fish-Slap Meeting

1. **Set the tone:** Start by being transparent. Let your team know that the purpose of this meeting is to get the stinky stuff out in the open and fix it together. Remind everyone of the "rules"—no blame or shame, specifics, and solutions (see the following #3 for more on this).

2. **Let it all hang out:** Give everyone a chance to voice their grievances, but keep it focused on one issue at a time. If someone throws a personal barb, intervene and say, "We're keeping it respectful." If someone veers off course, gently steer them back to the issue at hand.

3. **Don't rush to fix it (yet):** Sometimes, just airing out the issue is enough to make people feel heard and understood. Let the team get everything off their chest before jumping into solutions.

4. **Brainstorm:** Put the main issue themes up on a whiteboard or around the room and have people do a "gallery walk." This is something we did with clients at Deloitte, inviting them to put up sticky notes with new solutions to problems—or to add voting dots to suggested solutions.

5. **Close with action steps:** End the meeting by identifying clear next steps. What activities are the outcomes from today going to inform? What's the timeline for resolving the identified issues? How will you share how things are progressing?

The Magic of Regular Fish-Slapping

By holding these regular fish-slap sessions, you're patterning a culture of truth-telling, trust, and accountability. Just think, if a person feels comfortable speaking up, it's going to deepen the dialogue. It can strengthen relationships. It reduces the risk of misunderstandings turning into resentment. Plus, addressing issues early is like preventive maintenance for your team's morale. It's much easier to patch a small crack than to deal with a full collapse later.

So make space for that 10-day old carp. It may be uncomfortable at times, but a little discomfort now can save you from major troubles down the road.

Tip 4: Happy Workers Don't All Look the Same

When you picture an ambitious, engaged employee, what do you imagine? Is it someone striving for career advancement, "putting in the hours," and being vocal about wanting that promotion?

If so, it may be time for a good ol' dose of reality, no chaser. Employees today have wildly different motivations at work, ranging from those who want the "good-enough job" to those looking to climb fast and high, build a meaningful legacy, or work just enough to fund a life filled with travel, side hustles, or afternoon pickleball. People have different appetites for work responsibilities, career advancement, and the amount of their lives they want to invest in their jobs. As a leader, it's your responsibility to recognize that diversity in work styles and goals—and make it okay for employees to vary.

The Myth of the "One-Size-Fits-All" Worker

Here's the truth: No one wants to be a corporate robot. The "ideal" worker has long been portrayed as someone who eats, sleeps, and breathes their job, always available for overtime, and always reaching for the next rung up. But for some people, their job is just that: a job. They're perfectly happy working nine to five, delivering great work without the pressure to hustle 24/7. And that's more than okay—it actually looks a lot like balance to me.

On the other hand, some employees are hungry for more responsibility, want to take on stretch assignments, and will work extra hours, and that's okay too. You need to support that ambition without assuming everyone shares the same drive. Recognizing that people have different work appetites allows you to meet your team where they are. Only then can you help everyone thrive in their own way.

Ditch the Mold, Embrace the Individual

We've all been guilty of assuming things about people based on their work patterns. The person who stays late gets labeled as a go-getter. The one who leaves on time is often assumed to be disengaged. But guess what? Your assumptions are probably wrong.

Take a step back and check for any underlying assumptions you may have about the "right" way to work. Are you rewarding the person who works late, while overlooking the one who consistently meets their goals but leaves at five? People's professional choices don't always correlate with their level of happiness or commitment.

Similarly, not everyone lives the same kind of personal life, but everyone deserves to have theirs treated with the same level of respect. Just recently, while I was running a focus group assessing a company's culture, a frustrated young woman said, "I'm not a mom, but is my personal life any less important?" It was a powerful reminder that personal lives vary, and we can easily designate worthiness to one person's time spend while invalidating another. Some people have kids, others care for aging parents, some pursue degrees or hobbies, and others need time to recharge however they see fit. All of it matters, and all of it is worthy of respect.

Model and Respect Different Work Lifestyles

As a leader, your example decides whether there's respect for diverse lifestyles. Be open about your own boundaries, and encourage your team to set theirs. That might sound like "I'm logging off early to catch my kid's soccer game," or "I've blocked Friday mornings for deep focus on my development goals," or "Let's figure out a schedule that works with your caregiving needs."

If you create space for your team to bring their fully human selves to work, they'll feel supported and energized—whether they're at the office every day or only once a week.

Celebrate the Variety

The key to a healthy, high-performing team is recognizing that happiness doesn't look the same for everyone. Encourage team members to communicate their needs and expectations around work. Some may want more facetime with you, while others might prefer more flexibility. Allow for these differences and make room for them in your team culture.

How? Fortunately you don't need a crystal ball or this month's horoscope—just ask! Make a point of asking your team members about their preferred working style. You could ask, "How do you work best?" "What does a productive day look like for you?" or "What kind of support from your manager helps you do your best work?" Then take notes so you can reference what you learn.

A well-rounded team thrives on diverse work styles and goals. Support your team in finding their own paths to success, and watch them flourish.

Tip 5: Diverse Voices, Elevated Choices

Sameness is a silent killer. Just think, if your team thinks alike, talks alike, and nods in unison like dashboard bobbleheads, yikes! *You're in trouble*. A culture built on sameness breeds stagnation. Sure, harmony feels nice and pleasant, but in today's high-speed world, it can also be a fast track to irrelevance. That's because innovation happens not in echo chambers but when differing voices shake things up.

The Power of "Wait, What?!"

When someone on your team offers an idea that makes you pause and think, "Wait, what?!" pay attention. That moment of cognitive dissonance is gold. It's the friction and newness that spark creativity. *Welcome those moments*. Lean in. Ask follow-up questions. When my team makes a provocative suggestion, I'll say, "Oh, tell me more!" Even if my boss brain wants to stress-test the idea immediately, I try to stay open. Ideas that disrupt your assumptions or challenge the status quo? These are often the initial sparks of innovation.

Build a Culture of Constructive Collisions

In order to cultivate diverse perspectives, you have to create conditions for them to intersect and even collide productively. Start by asking:

- Who's *not* in the room? If everyone has similar backgrounds or viewpoints, you're missing out. Proactively invite people who see the world differently.

- Who's *not* speaking up? Silence doesn't mean agreement. Pay attention to who isn't contributing and create space for them. Try: "I'd love to hear your take—what's your perspective, Juan?" Sometimes the best ideas come from quiet voices.

- Who can play devil's advocate? Assign someone to challenge assumptions and offer opposing viewpoints. This prevents groupthink and ensures all angles are considered. It's also a really fun, low-risk way to normalize healthy debate.

Your Team Needs a Patchwork of Perspectives

Your team of strategists, builders, creatives, and analysts thrives because of the mix. Think of it like a patchwork quilt—each piece is storied and unique, vital for the contrast in brings. When diverse minds collaborate, they challenge assumptions, explore unconventional ideas, and find smarter solutions. They don't just survive change; they excel.

Here are questions you can ask next time you're staffing a project or team:

- Who thinks differently than I do?
- Who excels where we struggle?

- Who challenges the status quo on this?
- Who brings unexpected insights?

Change It Up

Beyond making sure you have the right people at the table, you can add practices that weave diverse perspectives into the fabric of your team. Try these moves to inspire more meaningful exchange on your team:

- **Rotate decision-making roles:** Switch up who leads meetings, presents proposals, or makes the final call. Even if you lead the meeting, assign agenda items to others.
- **Reverse mentorship:** Pair leaders with junior employees for two-way learning. This provides junior folks with a rich source of experience and wisdom and provides leaders with a direct line to the experiences and viewpoints of a significant portion of their workforce. Wisdom flows both ways.
- **Idea jams:** Hold brainstorming sessions where every idea must challenge the status quo. No "safe" suggestions allowed.
- **Feedback loops:** Regularly solicit anonymous team feedback on how inclusive the team, culture, and discussions feel—and act on it.

Teams with diverse perspectives work better and win bigger. Research consistently shows that diverse teams outperform homogeneous ones in profitability[3] and decision-making.[4] Why? Because they think wider, adapt faster, and solve deeper.

So next time you feel tempted to hire or collaborate with someone just because they're "a good culture fit," pause. Look for culture adders: people who stretch, improve, and amplify the team's thinking. Your future success depends on it!

Tip 6: Demonstrate Power-Sharing

There's this faulty leadership belief I see again and again: *The more you control, the more powerful you are.* We might think that making solo decisions, having the final say, or leading every meeting ourselves shows strength. But true power looks different from that. It's not desperate. Nor is it screaming, "Don't forget who's in charge here!" It comes from boosting others. Power-sharing—is the new power. It's an active choice on your part to distribute authority, empowering your team to take ownership, lead, and collaborate.

Power-Sharing: The Leadership Secret Weapon

When you share leadership responsibilities, everyone gets more opportunities to contribute, lead, and feel heard. But remember, not everyone expresses leadership in the same way. One team member might jump at the chance to run a meeting, while another prefers to share ideas in writing after thinking them through. Some may shine in one-on-one settings, others in group brainstorms or cross-functional projects. Power-sharing isn't one size fits all and that's okay.

Want to truly share power? Relinquish some decision-making downward so it doesn't sit only with you. See if you can push down "reward power" while you're at it, where you're not the only one calling out great behavior. Your team can use a mechanism like Shoutout Wednesdays to recognize the great work of others. And don't forget expert power. This is when you acknowledge someone's unique expertise and regularly defer to them on it. When done thoughtfully, these kinds of power-sharing build trust, help you and your team discover new talents, and show them that their voices don't simply matter—they're essential.

Rotate Facilitation Responsibilities

A simple way to demonstrate power-sharing is rotating facilitation responsibilities. Instead of one person leading every meeting, let different team members guide the agenda and lead discussions. This lightens your load and gives others the chance to develop leadership skills and build confidence. It also shows that their judgment and ideas matter, and it helps them appreciate the complexities of managing a team. *Empathy, anyone?*

By rotating facilitation duties, you also foster collaboration. Team members get to step up and feel more connected to the process that they're executing on. And you? You're guaranteed to get more fresh perspectives and creative solutions.

Give Spotlight Time to Each Team Member

Another key element of power-sharing is spotlight time. Allocate specific moments in meetings for each person to share updates, thoughts, or insights—without interruptions or multitasking. This practice reinforces everyone's being valued and heard. And it encourages quieter team members to find their voice and contribute meaningfully. On that note, make sure to give your team members advance notice (and the opportunity to say "no thanks"). *Because nobody likes that feeling of being suddenly pushed onto the stage like it's their turn at karaoke.* Some will feel ready and willing if they have time to prepare, while others might prefer to shine via written contributions that you or another team member can share on their behalf.

A former boss did this for me once, asking me to present to my team four learnings from a conference I attended. He not only boosted me in that moment by making the suggestion, but carrying through with it made it at least 50% easier for me to contribute ideas to my team in the future. After all, if you can't practice having a voice on your team, where else can you practice expressing yourself?

Celebrate Growth, Not Just Results

As you share power, acknowledge your people: the courage it takes to lead a meeting for the first time or present an idea, the hard call they had to grapple with and make on a project decision, their willingness to stand in the spotlight and be visible for the first time. Every leadership opportunity is a chance to develop and build confidence— and to meet it with a learning mindset.

Power to the People

Leadership shines brightest when it's shared. Power-sharing builds a culture of trust, collaboration, and mutual respect. Give your team the reins 20% more than you think you should, and watch them exceed expectations.

Tip 7: Meeting Norms: Energizers, Engagement, and Emoji Face

A great meeting can be a powerhouse of productivity. (Nothing like a looming deadline and a tray of leftover muffins to get two people to draft a report in 24 minutes flat.) But at their worst, meetings are like a glorified nap session with half the room zoning out and the other half secretly checking emails under the table. How do you change the mood and make meetings a place people want to show up to?

It's all about practicing meeting norms that keep energy high, engagement strong, and the overall experience one where you want to show up again. That'll boost productivity, but also make meetings more enjoyable, collaborative, and easy.

Set Clear Expectations

Before hitting "Join Meeting," make sure everyone knows what to expect. Think beyond an agenda: How should participants engage? Companies like Google, Microsoft, and Amazon have written meeting norms emphasizing clear communication and ask for active participation. At Atlassian, they expect meetings to have a defined purpose and encourage contributions from everyone. Let your team know if the meeting is open for all voices or is more informational with time for questions at the end. By communicating expectations upfront, you minimize confusion, blurt-outs, and awkward silences. And by creating clear norms for all, you make it easy to reward great behavior (and use common language to address the bad).

Meetings Need to Be Minimal

No shockers here, but excessive meetings lead to disengagement and burnout. So treat meetings like your finest china and use them minimally! If it can be done asynchronously, skip the meeting.

Encourage your team to reflect on whether meetings could be replaced by emails or quick check-ins. A culture that values minimal, meaningful meetings helps respect your team's time. Plus it prevents burnout, helping people engage fully when they do meet.

Equal Regard for Remote and In-Person Employees

In hybrid meetings, try to make sure all employees—whether remote or in-person—are treated equally. To ensure everyone feels seen and included, be mindful of nonverbal cues like someone leaving for extended periods or looking totally blank. Notice when a few people in the same room engage in a slightly quiet sidebar conversation about the meeting topic, then intervene; have them update the group or invite them to join back in. A great leader gives equal attention to both sets of employees during meetings so no one's left out of discussions. This is subtle to most employees, but it does avoid the feeling of insiders and outsiders among hybrid teams.

Emoji Face: Keeping the Energy Alive

Virtual meetings have a way of flattening people's affect—partly because we can't see all their body language cues and partly because we're interacting with a screen, not the real person. But you can liven virtual meetings up by adopting what I call "Emoji face." This means you purposefully use facial expressions and gestures to show engagement over the screen—a quick smile, a thumbs up, or an excited look of surprise communicates more than words. Leaders who show engagement set the tone for others to follow. Just think, if you're connected, "up," and energized by the future, your team will probably mirror that.

I can remember the first virtual talk I gave at an insurance company after the pandemic started. It felt like speaking into a void: no audience feedback, no energy bouncing back. I knew I had to adjust fast to keep things engaging, so I started incorporating more facial expressions and gestures, making sure to smile and nod (or even scowl if the anecdote or story fit) at the right moments. It felt oddly theatrical and over the top at first, but the more I did it, the more I noticed others started responding in kind, with loosened up energy—giving a thumbs up, clapping emojis, and raised hands. The energy in the virtual room shifted. Use that! Build in purposeful moments of interactivity. Plant something in your slides people aren't expecting—whether poignant, humorous, or just oddball. Plan to show your message, not just tell it, so they stay with you.

Create a Culture of Engagement

You can encourage the kind of participation where everyone talks by asking open-ended questions or using quick polls. I like to start these out really easy and accessible, such as "What's one word that comes to mind when you think of our business development process/marketing innovations/community outreach?" and then if needed, ask more layered questions after people have warmed up, like "Which of these factors do you believe is most important to our client prospects/ buyers/community members?" Incorporating these practices helps everyone contribute, even in remote settings, and creates a more vocal and inclusive environment. Win!

Keep Meetings Actionable

Out brains love to jump to the future. Before you're even done you're current project status update, people are wondering what's ahead. So end your meetings making sure everyone knows the next steps. Recap key decisions, assign owners, and confirm deadlines out loud so there's no confusion. Bonus points if you end with a quick check-in: "Is everyone clear on what's next?" or "Any blockers we should flag now?" That way, people leave feeling not just informed, but energized and ready to take action.

Meetings don't have to be a drag. You just need a little planning, a little energy and presence, and maybe one less spreadsheet. Keep it focused, human, and worth showing up for.

Tip 8: Delegate Like a Boss

Raise your hand if you've ever been overwhelmed with a pressing task but thought, "You know what? It'll be easier if I just do it myself." Relatable (I know I'm guilty!), but this default-thinking flushes time-savings right down the toilet. It leads to burnout, missed growth opportunities for your team, and a drop in the quality of work. Plus, you end up wasting (poorly allocated) time and disengage your team in the process. But the upside? It's major: one Gallup study found that CEOs who excel in delegating generate 33% higher revenue and report significantly faster company growth.[5]

Delegation isn't all or nothing, even if most of us treat it like a relay race—where you either pass the baton completely or clutch it for dear life and sprint the whole thing yourself. In reality, delegating is about finding that just-right balance of involvement, knowing when to step in and when to step back, and adjusting your level of engagement to make sure the task is completed efficiently and effectively. Sharpening your delegation skills is going to empower your team to take ownership, build confidence, and free up your time for strategic priorities.

The secret? Learning to stop thinking in terms of black and white (*should I or shouldn't I delegate*) and start choosing the distinct level of involvement you need for the situation at hand. There, you adjust based on the complexity of the task and the experience of the person taking it on. Done right, you're communicating, "I understand different projects call for different levels of support," "I trust you" and "I'm encouraging your growth." When you delegate effectively, you're not only multiplying your output but also positioning your team for success.

Next time you delegate, identify what level of ownership matches the task—and be sure to communicate that.

Level 1: Directive Delegation—"Do Exactly This"

When speed and precision matter, be clear and specific. Think of this level like assembling flat-pack IKEA furniture: Follow the instructions step by step. Example: "Draft this report using last quarter's template, and email it to me by Friday." This level is ideal when the task requires minimal decision-making and clear instructions to avoid errors.

Level 2: Guided Delegation—"Here's the Framework"

Provide direction but let the team member fill in the details. Example: "Create a social media calendar for next month. Use past campaigns as a guide, and flag any new ideas for my input." This approach is effective when you want your team member to take ownership but still need to ensure alignment with a set goal or standard.

Level 3: Collaborative Delegation—"Let's Tackle This Together"

Work alongside your team member, sharing responsibility. This level is great for coaching or when a task has high stakes. Example: "Let's draft the project proposal together. You take the first stab at the outline, and we'll refine it together." It allows you to guide while still empowering the individual to contribute their ideas and insights.

Level 4: Consultative Delegation—"Bring Me Recommendations"

Ask your team member to research, analyze, and suggest solutions. You make the final decision based on their input. Example: "Research three potential vendors for our new software platform and recommend the best fit based on cost and features." This level provides your team with the autonomy to gather information and present options but still leaves you with the final say.

Level 5: Full Ownership—"You've Got This"

Hand over the reins entirely when trust and expertise are high or experimentation is appropriate. Check in only for updates or when critical decisions arise. Example: "You're in charge of the decision-making and execution of the product launch event. Let me know if you hit any roadblocks." This level requires you to have a high level of trust in your team member's skills and judgment. At this stage, your involvement should be minimal because they are fully equipped to take ownership of the task. Your role now is less project emcee, more enthusiastic audience member.

I'll never forget how, as a new manager, I once thought I was giving Level 2 instructions for a client event, only to realize I was unintentionally assigning Level 5 ownership. The team chose and quickly locked in a venue that felt trendy and cool but turned out to be too loud and raucous for our client crowd. The result? A chaotic dinner where no one could hear each other over the crowd, and our seated guests had an unintentional front-row view of bar patrons' backsides as people packed in nine-deep for a drink. It was a good reminder: Clear communication about ownership can make all the difference.

Delegating across a spectrum can help you hold the reins when you need 'em and let them go when it's someone else's turn. Master these five levels and you'll empower your team while reclaiming time for the leadership work that only you can do. Less micromanaging, more momentum.

Tip 9: Check-Ins over Check-Ups: Ask How People Are Doing—Genuinely

Look, nobody loves hearing "How's it going?" if it's in a mechanical, "Just checking if your report is on schedule" kind of thing. That's not a check-in. That's a check-up. Check-ups feel a lot like micromanagement—where bosses need to monitor work or confirm completion. But employees can easily sense that the whole point is to verify work done, not to connect with the person behind the task. *Yawn.*

Now, a check-in is a whole other ballgame. It's human. You're checking in to see how someone's feeling about the workload, how their brain is holding up, and whether they feel supported—not *just* whether they're hitting their numbers. You're actually showing up for them above and beyond the task at hand.

Why Check-Ups Are the Fast Track to Burnout

Studies show that when leaders make the effort to ask, "How are you?"—and truly mean it—it can significantly reduce stress and anxiety among employees. And a McKinsey & Company study found that leaders who offer emotional support through regular check-ins help reduce work-related stress by as much as 33%.

It's also about fostering a culture of care and mutual respect. People who feel trusted and supported are more likely to take initiative and perform well under pressure too. Now who doesn't want that?!

How to Make the Shift: Prioritize the Person, Not Just the Task

Ready to move from check-ups to check-ins? Here's how you do it:

1. **Ask "How are you really doing?"** And no, don't just ask it like a throwaway question. Ask because you care. Ask, "How's the workload feeling?" or "What support do you need from me to make sure you don't lose your mind this week?" It's about the whole person, not just their to-do list.

2. **Listen like you actually care.** You've asked how they're doing— now *really* listen. Like, ears fully tuned, email minimized, and your "uh-huh" meter turned off. Acknowledge what they're telling you before problem-solving: "Yes, I can see how it would be stressful to lead this project on top of that deadline that got moved." Or you can validate their point of view by saying, "This project's been a real beast, huh? You've had everything thrown at you."

3. **Don't just listen—act.** A check-in isn't a one-way street. If someone shares they're drowning in work, step up and help them out. If they're struggling, help them find a solution. (Hint: It's probably not just "working harder.") Maybe that means offering them a project co-lead, helping with time management, or maybe just giving them a mental health day. People need to know that when they're heard, something changes.

Make It a Habit, Not a Once-in-a-While Thing

Check-ins boost morale, reduce turnover, and can seriously level-up team dynamics. When you prioritize them, you're showing your team that you care about their well-being and not just their output. They'll feel supported, seen, and valued. And guess what? They'll work harder for you because they know you're invested in their good, not just their ability to churn out reports.

If you want to create a thriving culture, check-ins can't be a one-time thing. Don't wait for a crisis to check in on people. Make it a habit—daily or weekly—so that it feels natural when things get tough.

The Power of Genuine Check-Ins: No Faking Allowed

Remember an important guardrail: Don't ask if you're not ready to listen—or better yet, act. When you take the time to truly engage and people feel it, you strengthen relationships and inspire trust and loyalty that goes beyond the surface. So *check in. Build the connection. Make people feel valued.*

3 Communication That Connects

Real talk builds real teams. Without communication, a team can feel like a group of strangers trying to solve a puzzle—except it's missing half the pieces, and the ones that are there are from a completely different puzzle altogether. Sounds chaotic, right?! But that's exactly what happens when we don't share, ask, or clarify along the way.

Now picture this instead. When communication flows freely, it sparks innovation, drives collaboration, and keeps things running smoothly, *even when the puzzle somehow turns into a Rubik's Cube halfway through!* A team that talks, listens, and adapts together can turn an idea into action, and a problem into an opportunity.

This chapter is all about when and how to share your message. This isn't about delivering vague platitudes or top-down announcements with no space for exchange. It's about saying what you mean in a way that opens ears and catalyzes dialogue. Whether you're in a brainstorming session, giving feedback, or even sending an email, your words need to land—not just sound good. In this chapter, you'll learn how to break down barriers with empathy and inclusiveness, and how to encourage your team to be just as bold with their communication. No more waiting for the "perfect" moment to say something. Let's make the most of every opportunity to connect with people and make sure everyone feels like they're on the same page.

Ready to speak in a way that actually gets people listening? Let's dive in. Because when communication flows, so does everything else.

Tip 1: Cut the Fluff and Say What You Mean

In a workplace humming with jargon and corporate speak, it's easy to fall into the trap of using safe, meaningless phrases. Words like "synergy," "pivot," or "circle back" are familiar (and plenty overused!), but think about it—they don't really say much. Do you want your team to have to "read the tea leaves" or use an app to translate your message? Of course not; they deserve better than that. They need clarity and direct communication that cuts through the noise.

Using clear, honest language is like giving your team a clear window to your thoughts, rather than leaving them guessing. It doesn't take an advanced degree to understand what's being said, it just takes a leader willing to be open and direct. And when people know where they stand with you, that critical thing called trust follows.

Round Edges Are for Furniture, Not Conversations

I get it—sometimes you might feel the urge to soften your words to keep the peace or avoid confrontation or a strong reaction from the other person. But here's the issue: "rounding off" your message only creates confusion. It doesn't make things comfortable; it just leads to misunderstandings.

For plenty of us, this becomes so normalized at work, it's an ingrained (unquestioned) habit. I used to be so fluent in corporate speak as a management consultant that once, on a Saturday hike with my husband and young twins, I caught myself saying, "We need to accelerate the path forward, leverage our daylight hours, and start optimizing our route." They stared at me, clueless, and it took a moment to realize how absurd I sounded. *Guess "Let's hurry before it gets dark" just doesn't have the same oomph!*

Think about it: Would you rather communicate, "We need to recalibrate our approach to drive greater synergy," or, "Our plan isn't working, so we need to rethink it"? The second one is clearer, more direct, and will spark action. So skip the corporate jargon, and get straight to the point.

Corporate Shorthand? Never Heard of It

Jargon sneaks in, and while a little might be unavoidable, too much only masks your true message. It can make you look like you're trying to sound smart, usually in a contrived way. Or you might sound like you're hiding behind buzzwords. So when you're writing or thinking through talking points, make an effort to say it plainly. Before delivering any message, ask yourself: *What's the simplest, most understandable way to say this?*

When you speak simply and directly, you show respect for *their* time and cognitive energy. You value your team enough to keep things clear and efficient, modeling that they too should prioritize accessible language, so no one's left behind.

And bonus tip, I've often mentally translated work jargon into what I'd say to a kid or a total industry outsider. If I can't explain it simply, it's probably not clear enough for my team either. Try putting your message through the "kid test."

A Culture of Honesty Starts with You

It's easy to rely on jargon or avoid tough conversations, but as a leader, you set the tone. When you model transparency and honesty—no sugar-coating or corporate-speak—your team will follow suit. *(And imagine the collective sigh of relief when they actually understand what you mean the first time. No "synergistic paradigm shifts" needed!)*

Conversations will become more efficient, and trust in you will grow. You'll be known as someone who's direct, grounded, and unafraid to handle tough issues head-on.

Speak Human

At the end of the day, your team is made up of people who want to connect, understand, and do their best. They want to know what's going on, what's expected of them, and how they're contributing. When you cut out vague speak, you get more authentic, meaningful conversations.

So next time you catch yourself complicating a message, try "Let me rephrase that without the jargon," or "Let me simplify that—sometimes I get carried away," and reset the conversation. Cut the fluff, speak human, and your team will thank you.

Tip 2: Speak the Language of Equals

You know the saying "It's not what you say, it's how you say it"? Well, in leadership, it's definitely what you say *and* how you say it. Your words have the power to shape how your team feels—whether that's valued and heard, or like they're simply there to carry out your grand vision. (And we definitely don't want anyone getting that "barking orders" feeling.)

That's why I'm challenging you to speak the language of equals. When you do, you instantly shift the power dynamic. Instead of "I'm in charge, so do this!" you're saying, "We're in this together. Let's make it happen!" And that little change in language? It makes a world of difference.

Why Language Matters

The words you choose send a powerful message about how you view your team. Do you see them as collaborators, equals, or order-takers? By making a point to choose words that emphasize that they have say-so, power, and autonomy, just like you, you make people feel like they have some control and stake in the future. Here are ways to do it:

- Swap "I need you to …" with "Can you take the lead on …?"
- Acknowledge expertise: "You know this best—what's the best approach?"

- Replace directives with collaboration: "Let's tackle this together."
- Say "How do you see it?" instead of assuming alignment.
- Shift from authority to partnership: "What do you need from me to make this a success?"

This shift in framing your message is a form of power-sharing (*the opposite of power-hoarding!*) And it's a conscious choice to elevate their role and importance.

Swap "I" for "We"

If you've ever caught yourself saying, "I've decided we're going with this strategy," or even "I want that by Monday morning," it's time for a more modern approach. *Remember, we're focused on people-first leadership here!* A big part of that is involving people in decisions that affect them. For example, instead of saying, "I've decided we're going with this strategy," try "How do we feel about this strategy as a team?" Instead of saying, "I want that by Monday morning," try "Ideally we can aim for Monday, but let's look at what's realistic for the team." As a leader, you don't need to carry everything on your shoulders. In fact, speaking in the "we" is a subtle but powerful way to share ownership and empower your team. And don't worry. You're not passing off responsibility. You're inviting people into the process and giving them a stake in the outcome.

When you use "we," you're acknowledging that every member of the team is integral to the mission. You're signaling that you're all in this together. Plus, it helps prevent you from slipping into the mindset of "I'm in charge … I'll decide … I have all the answers." *Spoiler alert: You don't!*

Invite Input, Don't Issue Orders

Have you ever felt like you were responding to a command from a boss, where you were the equivalent of Siri, rather than engaging in a human conversation? *That's the furthest thing from collaboration!* Instead of telling people what to do, try asking for input. Use phrases like "What do you think about this idea?" or "How do you see us approaching this challenge?" It shifts the power dynamic and invites others to contribute, while also showing you value their perspective.

This recognizes that your team is a wellspring of ideas and expertise. So lean in and listen. People respect leaders who ask for their input and act on it.

Your Brain Isn't the Only Good One Here

Help people feel heard, and you help them feel valued. By being mindful of your words and making simple swaps in your language to share power and influence over the future, you'll create a team dynamic where trust, respect, and collaboration thrive—because you're not just the boss. You're a partner in a shared mission, working alongside people who want to feel like they matter.

So next time you're about to issue a royal decree, remember: A little partnership goes a long way.

Tip 3: Active Listening Is the Real Power Move

Let's talk about a superpower you might be underutilizing: listening. It's easy to think you're doing it. Maybe you're nodding along, tossing in an "Uh-uh, totally" here and there, all while mentally drafting your next brilliant point. We've all been there.

But true *active* listening? It requires letting the other person feel like the main character in the conversation, not just a competing voice trying to break through the noise of your inner monologue.

When you show up like that? People open up. They bring ideas, concerns, and creative sparks they'd otherwise keep to themselves. When you master this, you'll see your team thrive in ways you didn't expect.

The Power of Whole-Body Listening

Just like my twins learned in the third grade, active listening is a full-body experience. If you've ever poured your heart out to someone who was half-checking their phone, you know the joy of competing for attention with a phone's digital chirps! On the flip side, I think of my mentor, Simon Bailey, who models a totally different kind of listening. When you talk to him, it's like he's placed a temporary "Do Not Disturb" sign on his entire being. He leans in so intently I half-expect him to pull out a magnifying glass. He listens with his eyes, his body, and his mind, making you feel seen and heard. After experiencing that, I realized how much I needed to level-up my own listening game, and it changed how I show up in conversations.

Acknowledge, Don't Interrupt

Building on that idea of making someone feel heard, let's talk about a major communication pitfall: interruptions. Interruptions are one of the biggest trust-breakers in communication, even if they come from a place of "Oh, that reminds me!" (enthusiasm) or "Gotta jump in quick" (urgency). When you become aware of your urge to jump in, and shift it to acknowledgment—not interrupting or sidelining—it shows respect and builds connection. A simple acknowledgment like "I hear you, Tom," or "Shamika, that's a great point," sends a powerful message: I value what you're saying, and I'm listening. These small affirmations pave the way for deeper, more meaningful discussions. They also give you a replacement for talking over others with less-than-helpful phrases like "What you're trying to say is …" or "Oh that reminds me, [insert totally different subject]"!

To take it further, try reflecting back what you've heard as a thoughtful summary. You might say, "It sounds like you're suggesting we rethink the timeline because of the upcoming deadline," or "I hear that you're frustrated with the lack of communication in the process." This helps the other person feel understood and can clear up misunderstandings.

And if you truly sense the person is stifling their real feelings about something, excavate it. As Amy Gallo, a contributing editor at *Harvard Business Review*, advises, asking questions about what may have been left unsaid can make the other person feel supported and lead to insights for both parties. For instance, if a colleague mentions, "I'm worried about my presentation for the board meeting," instead of offering generic reassurance, you might respond, "I was nervous when I started presenting too. What's worrying you?"[1] By adopting these active listening techniques, you create an environment where team members feel heard, valued, and understood, fostering trust and open communication.

Nonverbal Cues Matter Too

Your body language also speaks volumes. Lean forward, maintain steady eye contact, and heck, put down your coffee cup if you need to! Even small gestures like nodding or uncrossing your arms can signal that you're engaged and open. When I need to activate my own attention—don't laugh—I channel my inner detective: I square up to my counterpart and take in every detail with rapt attention just like a detective doing an interview, as though I don't want to miss a thing. These nonverbal cues, which signal "generous listening," often say more than words ever could.

Leading by Listening

Unfortunately, feeling overlooked is relatively common. Active listening cuts through noise, showing people that their ideas and time matter. And that person who feels heard is more likely to contribute creatively and work collaboratively. They're more likely to bring their best selves to the table because they know their voice counts.

I can't overstate the ripple effect of active listening. It builds trust, strengthens relationships, and fosters an environment where solutions emerge faster and more effectively.

Listening isn't flashy, but it's one of the most powerful leadership tools at your disposal. So next time you're in a meeting, try listening more than you speak. You might be surprised at the insights that unfold—insights you'd have missed entirely otherwise.

Tip 4: The Three-Sentence Rule: Be Quick, Be Brilliant, Be Gone

Did I ever tell you about the time I tried to impress a particularly influential executive at my company? He reached out with a request, and despite being stuck in the Chicago O'Hare airport, I crafted a thorough reply, then promptly hit send. The problem? I wrote the entire thing in the subject line.

Nooooo! I was so mortified I practically expected the airport PA system to announce my monumental blunder right there in Terminal 2.

That's how *not* to send an email.

The good news is that there are guideposts that can help you avoid email mishaps like mine—or email becoming a soul-sucking time thief. (*Because hey, if your team spends more time skimming emails than acting on them, it's time to do something different*). Enter the Three-Sentence Rule, which, when it comes to your emails, empowers you to be clear, be concise, and be *done*.

Why Brevity Wins Every Time

Let's be honest—no one's yearning for another novel-length email clogging their inbox. Long-winded messages dilute your point, increase miscommunication, and slow decision-making. They can also make you appear out of touch with people's realities. Keeping it short forces clarity and respects everyone's time.

The Anatomy of a Great Three-Sentence Message

Here's the deal: 90% of your emails should follow the three-sentence rule. That means after your greeting, the meat of your message is about three sentences long. You need less than you think.

1. **Start with context.** Open with a clear reason for reaching out. Example: "I'm following up on yesterday's project meeting."
2. **State the ask or update.** Be specific about what you need or what's happening. Example: "We need your input on the budget allocation for next quarter."
3. **Add a call-to-action.** Tell them what's next. Example: "Please review the attached plan and let us know your input by Thursday."

Notice we're keeping the language nice and simple. That's because clear, straightforward language helps you come across as clearer and more approachable. Not just that, but it can actually make you appear smarter! Princeton University researcher Dr. Daniel Oppenheimer found that writers who use long words needlessly are seen as *less* intelligent than those who stick with basic vocabulary and plain text.[2]

When More Detail Is Necessary

Once in a while, three sentences won't cut it, and that's okay. Use bullet points or numbered lists to break up the content, keeping things digestible. If deeper context is needed, say, "Happy to provide more details or to send the full report."

What to Avoid Like the Plague

Sometimes "un-advice"—or what not to do is as helpful as positive guidance. Here are a few common email faux pas to look out for:

- **Vague subject lines:** "Quick Question" or "Important" tells people nothing.
- **Paragraph piling:** Dense, unbroken blocks of text create instant fatigue.
- **Multiple requests buried in one message:** Make it easy by sticking to one main ask.

Get to the Point Without Losing the Plot

Applying the Three-Sentence Rule means more action and less confusion. Your team will notice you respect their time. And next time you're crafting a message in a hurry—whether from an airport terminal or a coffee shop—you'll know exactly how to get your point across without writing a novel or clogging up the subject line!

Tip 5: Smile Before You Speak

Years ago, I worked with a senior partner at a consulting firm who had a reputation for making big swings that *always* seemed to pan out. Colleagues joked that everything she touched turned to gold. But here's what struck me most about her and it was more profound than it sounds: She was a smiler, and not in a silly or superficial way. Even over phone calls, you could *hear* her smile— her crackle and enthusiasm for what she was talking about and people *felt* it. That enthusiasm helped her build trust, inspire teams, and sell bold ideas with ease.

Why a Simple Smile Changes Everything

What's the fastest way to connect with others on a human level? Smile genuinely before you speak. If you're in the same room, it immediately signals your warmth, but even through the phone, when you're welcoming people and they can't see your face, they *can* hear and experience your positivity and sincerity.

Research shows that smiling triggers the release of dopamine, serotonin, and endorphins—the body's natural mood boosters. But here's the leadership twist: When *you* smile, your voice naturally sounds more engaging, welcoming, and sincere. It's not just psychological. It's physiological. People are wired to respond positively to warmth, making them more receptive to your ideas, feedback, and even tough conversations.

How to Use This in Real Life

You've got an important call coming up—let's say with a new client prospect your organization hopes to land. Before you hit the green phone icon, pause. Take a deep breath and genuinely smile (not a forced, photo-op grin from second-grade picture day), but the real thing. Then speak. Notice how your tone softens, your words flow better, and the bump *you* feel in confidence. It works just as well for in-person conversations and Zoom meetings—bonus points if they can see your smile, too.

When It Matters Most

- **Team check-ins:** Think about it: If you look like you're dragging yourself into a team meeting and your energy level is best described as "room temperature sloth," that's exactly how your team will behave. But on the other hand? Starting with warmth sets a positive tone in terms of morale that can be contagious.

It can transform a potentially draining check-in into an energizing and connecting moment.

- **Cross-team collaborations:** Chances are, you want to make a good impression with your partners and peers across the organization. By starting these interactions with a genuine smile, even when dealing with a contentious issue, it tells the folks in engineering you're not just there to point fingers at their latest bug, but to brainstorm solutions with a "We're all in this (leaky) boat together" mentality.

- **Presentations *and* pitches:** People don't just buy ideas—they buy into *you*. That's why even the glossiest pitch deck can't do what your smile does. Walk in with a smile that suggests you're genuinely excited to share, and your audience is way more likely to lean in and take interest.

But What About "Fake" Smiles?

You're right to side-eye any advice that implies you should "just smile more." Women in particular have been unfairly told to do so for generations. But I'm not asking you to perform happiness. If anything, part of shaping your own signature leadership style is to try out different methods that help you lead with warmth and authenticity. So to be extra clear: We're not advocating for a corporate-mandated, 24/7 "Miss America" smile. *Nope!* People can spot insincerity a mile away. The goal is to ground yourself in a genuine intention to connect. If you're not in the mood to smile, try a mindset shift: Focus on the positive impact your words could have, and let that intention bring a natural positivity to your expressions or gestures.

Your Leadership Homework

For the next week, try this experiment: Before every meeting or important conversation, pause, take a breath, and smile, genuinely. See how people respond differently. Notice how you *feel* different.

A smile before you speak might seem trivial, but in a world where workplace disillusionment runs high, small acts of warmth go a long way. Sometimes connection doesn't have to be that complicated.

Tip 6: Be the Bridge, Not the Bottleneck

If you've ever been on a project where you felt stuck, waiting on that one person to send the last email, share the missing data, or approve the final decision, you know how frustrating it can be. That feeling of waiting for the signal to go ahead is a productivity (and sometimes motivation) killer. When you're a leader, you do not want to be the person everyone's waiting on to move forward.

So who holds the power to break this cycle? Well, it's not the IT department, or your boss—ding, ding, ding … it's you! You can be the bridge that keeps communication flowing smoothly, not the bottleneck that clogs it up.

Stop Playing Gatekeeper (Like a Buckingham Palace Guard)

I once consulted for a retail company that was struggling to become a more innovative and efficient place to work. During our employee focus groups, we uncovered a major issue: a culture of excessive control (and bottlenecks). I'll never forget that the CFO had to approve an employee's request to order *Post-it Notes*. Yeah, you read that right. A single box of sticky notes had to go through the CFO's desk. As you can imagine, it wasn't just about office supplies. This bottleneck mentality permeated most processes, slowing everything down and stifling autonomy and ownership. By working on pushing responsibility and authority downward, that company was ultimately able to shift toward a culture of greater trust, faster decision-making, and more innovation.

Transparency: The Ultimate Trust Multiplier

It's problematic to hold things up, but a twin sin in leadership is actively hoarding information. When you keep crucial information to yourself, thinking you're protecting your influence or power, you're actually just making people wait. (Plus, you're making them more dependent on *you*.) The longer the wait, the more tension builds and, understandably, people get frustrated.

To be a people-first leader, you view information-sharing as something that promotes equity and respect among your team members. That means you share information openly and promptly. Not just the good stuff. Not just the pieces of data that make you look good. (This, of course, excludes confidential information like an employee's performance rating or sensitive internal investigations). The point is, if you're the person holding the key to something important, don't wait until the last minute to unlock it. Hand over that key ASAP and let your team move forward with the clarity they need.

Set the Example: Don't Be a One-Way Street

It's tempting, especially as a leader, to keep things close to the chest. A lot of the time, it feels like the "safe" route. But think about this: *Your team watches everything you do.* If you withhold information or power, they will take a cue to do it too. Shoot, they may even withhold information from each other! If you're transparent and communicative, they'll follow your lead.

It's time to let go of the illusion that you need to be the one with all the answers, keeping people waiting for your input. It's not about you; it's about the collective. To be the bridge and not the bottleneck, you have to embrace transparency in its fullest sense.

The more transparent you are, the more you'll notice that people don't need to depend on you for every little thing. They'll start owning more decisions on their own, driving the work forward without your every approval. That's how you create a team of leaders, not just followers.

Tip 7: Embrace Awkward Pauses

Whenever I lead workshops on self-advocacy, there's one exercise that consistently causes the most squirming, sweating, and downright discomfort. Asking participants to practice "strategic silence," where they pair up, lock eyes, and hold steady eye contact—without speaking. Within seconds, the air is pretty thick with antsy-ness. People fidget, glance away, and grimace nervously. Yet, by the end, they admit it was one of the most powerful lessons they've experienced.

Learning to get comfortable with silence is a secret weapon in your leadership toolkit. When you ask your team a question, this means you resist the urge to fill the space. Or when you're making an important request of your boss, you make the request, let it land, and don't rush to overexplain or babble through the void. An awkward pause might feel like standing in the middle of Times Square in your weirdest pajamas, but trust me, those silent seconds are where the magic happens.

Why We Fear Silence

Humans are wired to hate awkward pauses. We rush to fill them because silence can feel like a spotlight, highlighting our uncertainty or vulnerability. And I can't tell you how many well-intentioned people leaders do this, often without noticing. Leaders might give the team a prompt and then overcompensate, jumping in with answers, clarifications, or restatements before anyone has a chance to respond. The result? Meetings dominated by the loudest (and more senior) voices while thoughtful, reflective team members stay quiet.

The Richness of the Pause

In communication, silence is like rich soil—give it space, and ideas will sprout. When you ask a thoughtful question, hit the pause button. Count to five slowly in your head (it'll feel like an eternity, but it's not). Watch what happens next: someone will step into the silence with a deeper, more considered response than if you'd rushed to fill the gap. Just think: You wouldn't rush a prize-winning orchid, would you?! Same goes for a truly thoughtful response.

How to Make Silence Work for You

- **Set the expectation.** Normalize pauses by saying, "I'm giving everyone a moment to think before we respond." This frames silence as intentional, not weird or to be avoided.

- **Stay comfortable.** Practice holding silence in meetings until someone speaks. Breathe deeply to manage the discomfort.

- **Give yourself a set number of "speaking chips."** What if you limited yourself to a set number of speaking moments? This self-imposed limit forces you to be more intentional, concise, and impactful. Use them when your expertise or perspective is needed, and let others take the floor for routine updates. Consider saving your final chip for the meeting close to reinforce key points, inspire, or make a call to action.

- **Ask open-ended questions.** Avoid yes/no prompts. Use questions like "What possibilities haven't we explored yet?" or "How could we approach this differently?" These spark richer conversations.

What Silence Signals to Your Team

Pausing after a question shows that you value depth over speed. It tells your team you're not looking for the first answer—you're looking for *the best one*. This shift can transform discussions from surface-level chatter to meaningful collaboration. Plus, when you hold space for others to speak, you send a powerful message: "I trust you're intelligent enough to grapple with this and come up with an insight," even if it needs a beat to emerge. Respect grows when team members realize their thoughts are worth waiting for.

Flip the Script on Awkward

My former manager once asked my team and me a bold question: whether we should radically shift our approach on a project that had been a disaster up until then, letting go of old processes that weren't yielding results. We were exhausted, frustrated, and honestly, afraid to fail. No one knew how to respond to his question at first, and for a while it felt like we might just sit in that mud of uncomfortable silence forever. But once a single person voiced their concerns, it opened the door for a real, honest conversation that ultimately led to us changing things, and a much better solution.

Awkwardness is just the feeling of breaking old habits. Challenge yourself to reframe those moments of silence as productive tension— the kind that leads to breakthroughs.

Your Leadership Edge

Remember, silence isn't an absence of action. It's a powerful, intentional leadership move. Ready to embrace the pause? Go ahead—ask your next big question, and let the silence work its magic.

Tip 8: Speak to Execs Like a Journalist

Just like your team needs clarity and context, so does your manager. Most people assume forwarding updates or recapping your week is enough. But with this group in particular, you'll stand out if you deliver your message with clarity, brevity, and impact.

Senior executives, like you, are juggling competing priorities—but with an even broader lens and higher stakes. Their time is limited, and their focus is firmly on impact. If they had a dollar for every report or long email they've skimmed, they could probably fund the next big company initiative themselves.

To make sure your message resonates and drives action, you can learn a lot from the way journalists communicate. By thinking like a reporter, you craft messages that are sharp, purposeful, and cut through the noise, capturing the attention and prompting the support of those who matter most.

Speak in Headlines

In journalism, the headline is the sizzle—the sound that makes everyone stop and look, even before the steak hits the plate. It's the most important part of the story. It must grab attention, convey the essence of the message, and compel your listener to stay tuned in. So don't "bury the lede," as it's called, by moseying your way through a bunch of sentences to the big idea. Lead with the result or insight, getting straight to the point. Don't go into back story. For example, instead of starting with "In January, we began analyzing customer feedback and discovered several patterns along the way that could help improve the product," you might say, "Customer feedback shows three key product issues that are costing us $500K annually." The result or big punchline—what matters most—is immediately clear, and the rest can follow in more detail.

Serve the Insight Sandwich

If you have more time or interest from an executive than you anticipate, you can share extra information with the insight sandwich: Start with the key headline, insight, or takeaway, then layer in brief supporting data or context, and finish with a clear recommendation or action plan. So instead of presenting a laundry list of facts or chronological happenings they have to mentally sift through (*that'll drain someone's battery real quick*), you serve your information in three clear courses. For example, you might say, "Our analysis of customer feedback has uncovered three recurring product issues. That's contributing to an annual loss of $500K. We recommend reallocating resources to address these problems, which will drive significant improvements in customer satisfaction and retention." You're keeping it brief, which gives them a chance to react to a certain point or interject with a follow-up question.

Declutter Relentlessly

Simplicity is a great guideline for communicating with executives, but here's something else it does: it keeps you more easily focused on your messages (since there's less stuff to cram in and remember). Knowing that leaders are often bombarded with information, you're making every word you use serve a purpose, no filler. So, skip phrases like "just," "I believe," and "maybe" that soften and weaken your message and reduce its impact.

In fact, in my most popular video on TikTok (with over three million views), I offer some rewrites for popular but cluttered (and frankly powerless) phrases:

- ~~I just wanted to share~~ I wanted to share …
- ~~Does that make sense?~~ What are your thoughts?
- ~~I may be wrong, but~~ Here's what I know …
- ~~Sorry to bother you~~ When you have a moment, I'd like …
- ~~I hope that's okay~~ Thanks for considering.

Trade lengthy explanations for concise, fact-driven statements that communicate the essence of your message. It not only improves *their* understanding of what you said, but it can lift your self-confidence to be so verbally poised and direct. For example, instead of saying, "It seems like addressing these issues *could* help our bottom line, so if possible, *we could try* …" you could say, "Our analysis shows addressing these issues will improve our bottom line by \$500K annually." See how less is more here? Think like a bonsai master and prune your message; be ruthless in your editing.

Answer "So What?" Before They Ask

One of the most important questions an executive will have in response to any presentation or conversation is "So what?" In other words, why should they care about the information you're presenting? You can help them, and boost your own leadership, by making sure every point you make directly ties back to the business goal—whether that's revenue, risk, growth, or customer impact. Make the stakes clear. Show how solving a problem will contribute to the organization's success and make a measurable difference. A simple way to frame this is: "You might be wondering why *this matters/why act on this now/why our team should lead it.* Here's why *it's worth the investment/it's especially timely/our team is well-positioned to lead it.*" Preempt their questions and make it easy for them to say yes.

Close with a Call to Action

End every conversation with a clear next step. Think of it like my favorite course—a yummy dessert after a great meal—something that leaves them satisfied and convinced their investment was well worth it. For example: "We recommend reallocating \$200K to address product issues by Q2. Do we have your support to move forward?" A strong closing request makes it more likely they'll say "yes" and shows you're thinking strategically, not just reporting up. By channeling your inner journalist and speaking in headlines, decluttering your words, and ending strong, you'll turn your updates from "blah" to "whoa!" Concise, clear, and full of insights that matter.

Tip 9: Encourage Radical Candor

If you want your team to thrive, they need to be able to speak their minds—the full, unvarnished truth. When they do that, their feedback can spark real change and even some uncomfortable silences (*think of it as the sound of progress*). Radical candor means building a culture where feedback is allowed and expected. A place where someone can say, "I'm not sure that's the right call," and know they won't pay for it later. And here's the secret: It all starts with you.

The Secret Sauce to Real Talk

Radical candor is clarity served with care. It's feedback that's honest *and* human. Think of it as the Goldilocks zone of feedback: not too harsh, not too sweet, but just the right balance of directness and care. It's a form of honesty that drives improvement while still showing you give a damn.

And don't think this makes you blunt or rude! It means being honest in a way that's constructive and helps the team move forward—for example, saying, "The presentation was clear and well-supported, but the opening felt a little rushed. Let's discuss," rather than, "The presentation didn't quite land for me."

Create a Culture of Trust and Openness

When we're worried we'll be ridiculed or retaliated against for speaking up, we humans tend to retreat. And that's where problems begin. If your team is hesitant to share their thoughts, you're risking burnout, disengagement, and frustration. People will begin to feel like their perspectives are inconvenient or unwelcome. For instance, if your teammate Liz quietly worries about a looming team deadline, but fears being seen as negative for voicing it, that concern festers; instead of being addressed, it could potentially lead to missed milestones and a rushed, lower-quality final product, not to mention crummy morale and reinforcing a pattern of people holding back their thoughts and opinions. Cultivating trust—being a people-first leader—calls on you to model vulnerability, openness to feedback, and practicing candor yourself.

The Power of Congruence

Don't ask for radical candor if you're not willing to work at it yourself. Your team is always watching you. If you're avoiding tough conversations, sugarcoating issues, or making passive-aggressive comments behind closed doors, you're setting a poor example. And they will most certainly notice.

That's why you need to be the first one to communicate in this way: Care personally, challenge directly. You're going beyond being direct, you're pairing that directness with a path forward. For example, instead of saying, "That presentation was a mess," try "You have great content, but it was hard to follow. Let's work on improving the flow for next time." That's clear, direct, and it provides a way to improve.

I once saw my former leader preach radical candor but avoid offering direct feedback when it was needed. After my colleague James gave us all a quick dry-run of his upcoming client presentation, it was clear it wasn't up to par. But our manager gave him a breezy, vague "blessing" and moved on. It wasn't until James went to our boss afterward for a follow-up question that the real concerns came out—by then, it was almost too late to make changes. *Ugh*. It was a stark reminder that if you want to foster radical candor, you need to model it by giving clear, actionable feedback right away.

Give Your Team the Tools to Thrive

Saying, "We value honesty" will only get you so far. You need to show your teammates how to give feedback in a way that promotes growth and collaboration.

Start by holding regular feedback sessions where team members can offer insights to one another. Make feedback part of the culture by introducing simple "sentence starters" that facilitate expressing concerns constructively or giving someone recognition. Examples include:

- "I appreciate how you ..."
- "Can I offer a suggestion that might help?"
- "One thing I'd change is ..."
- "I'm curious if you've considered ..."
- "It might help if we ..."
- "A tweak that might strengthen this is ..."
- "Here's something that tripped me up a bit ..."
- "This part landed really well. Here's why ..."

These phrases help frame feedback in a way that encourages open, solution-oriented conversations.

Radical Candor Means Facing the Hard Stuff

Okay, nobody loves being the bearer of bad news, but that silence that settles over your team when something feels off? It isn't peace. It's a quiet brew of unspoken anxieties and restless tensions. Radical candor asks leaders to *be the first* to break that tension by intervening with an honest observation—even about the "rub" between team members. That brief "Hey team, let's pause here.... I'm noticing X.... Can we talk about it?" is a sign of care, not criticism. It's time to normalize the discomfort of truth-telling by showing it's the only way to shared understanding and progress. When a leader models this brave vulnerability, it sends a powerful message: "We're all here to grow, and that means being honest, even when it's not easy." Silence stagnates; candor ignites.

4 Make Work Meaningful

You've probably heard it a gazillion times: "People are more motivated when they see purpose in their work." It's true—but it's also a lot easier said than done. It's not enough to slap some corporate mission statement on a wall or have a milestone celebration once a year and expect employees to feel connected. In reality, people want to know that their everyday progress matters. They want to see how their work contributes to something bigger than just ticking off to-do lists, fulfilling vague corporate goals, or helping the company earn more profits or status. (I mean, how many logoed golf tees or water bottles do we need before we all collectively snap!?)

So let's have a reset. This chapter dives deep into the magic of purpose at work. We'll explore how to transform mundane tasks into meaningful contributions, and I'll show you how to maximize the individual strengths each person brings to the table. Because—*real talk time*—if people can't connect their day-to-day work to a bigger picture, burnout and disengagement are right down the hall. Trust me, nobody is signing up for a motivational mouse pad with *Grind Through the Burnout* on it.

The best part? Creating this sense of meaning can happen one small moment at a time—through trust, consistency, and real-time proof points that someone's work matters (not so much through a grandiose speech or one-off "Purpose Day"). It's about finding the little ways to communicate why what we do matters—like sharing an email from a grateful customer or spotlighting how someone's leadership of an employee resource group (ERG) not only made employees feel seen but also sparked some new company-wide conversations. Weave in purpose—on purpose—and you're creating a culture where people feel respected, seen, and valued for the unique contributions they make every day.

Ready to roll up your sleeves and make work something people actually care about? Let's dig in.

Tip 1: Explain the Why

There's a power to purpose. It might sound like a throwaway buzzword (and, yes, entire books and business fads have been dedicated to it), but let's take a moment to verify this truth: *People are way more motivated when they understand the Why behind their work.* By contrast, assigning tasks and assuming everyone just "gets it" is like giving someone a map with no destination. You'll end up with people feeling unmoored, unfocused, and unsettled! Team members want to know their work isn't just busywork; it's helping to build something bigger. When they see how their efforts connect to a larger goal, motivation picks up naturally. But it's your job to be the bridge—to ensure that purpose is clear and meaningful for your team.

The Disconnect: Don't Assume They Just Get It

Ever had that moment where, in the middle of a project, someone asks, "Why are we doing this again?" (Or frankly, maybe you've had that thought yourself.) If your first thought is "Isn't it obvious?" you're not alone, but you're also not helping your team. The Why is rarely as obvious as we think it is.

Failing to communicate the purpose behind a project or initiative can make your team feel like they're just spinning their wheels. No one enjoys working for the sake of working. Think about it: if you're building a training website, you're writing code, designing pages, and making sure everything works. But *why* you're doing it might be to facilitate peer-to-peer learning and support, enhance user accessibility, and create a community space for shared experiences. That's the type of information that sparks passion. When people see the human impact of their work, they feel a sense of pride and ownership.

Share the Bigger Picture

So how can you communicate this "why"? A little transparency goes a long way. Don't just tell people what to do; explain why it matters and how their contributions fit into the larger picture. Providing context gives people clarity and motivation.

For example, instead of just saying, "We need to add the updated metrics to the report and get it out the door," try saying, "This report will help our leadership team make a crucial decision for the next quarter, which will shape how we support our customers moving forward. Your analysis is key in helping them understand the data and make informed decisions."

The value here is that we're showing the bigger impact. These simple sentence starters can help you zoom out the lens and explain the Why:

- "Think about the bigger picture. By doing this, we're …"
- "This work isn't just about hitting a deadline. It's about …"
- "Your contribution will have a huge impact on …"
- "The reason we're focusing on this is because …"
- "This project is important because it will help us …

A Little Goes a Long Way

Now, I'm not saying you need to give a 30-minute TED Talk every time you assign a task. No long, drawn-out lectures needed. But I am asking you to weave the Why into assigning tasks day to day—or encouraging someone who's in the middle slog of a tough project— and of course reviewing outputs at the end.

Communicating the Why is an ongoing practice. Regular check-ins and context-sharing show your team that their efforts matter. If you do this right, you won't have to worry about team motivation. Your people will be the first ones to step up and give their best.

Wrap It Up with the Why

Giving people a sense of meaning in their work is what separates getting the job done from doing it with passion. The Why turns a task into a mission.

As you master your own signature leadership style, connect the dots for people, and your team will have the clarity—and motivation—to push through even the toughest challenges.

Tip 2: Craft Their Growth Journey

In an age where burnout is rampant and career growth can feel slower than my first-apartment dial-up internet connection, it's time to rethink how we approach leadership and team development. People—especially Gen Z and Millennials—want progression. For a leader, one of your most powerful tools is helping your team members carve out a growth path that feels meaningful—not just for them, but for the organization. Now here's what some managers I coach don't like to hear: Their growth journey shouldn't be confined to your team. In fact, if you support their development—even if it means they'll eventually leave your department—you'll create loyal, high-performing employees who often become lifelong connections, resources, and maybe even your peers!

It's Not Just About Moving Up

We used to think of career growth as racking up new titles as you step up the corporate ladder. More and more, though, it's being shaped by gaining new skills, tackling different challenges, or even moving to a new department or role. You don't want to be the boss who sees employees only as "tools" to meet goals; no one likes being a spoke in a machine. So co-develop growth plans with your people. Make them personalized. Not only will your team members feel valued, you'll help them recognize their potential, even beyond their current role.

Will they outgrow their current position and leave? Maybe. And that's okay. But again, when you invest in their growth, you build loyalty that goes beyond paychecks or titles.

Talk About Their Last Day on Their First Day

Imagine you're in your very first meeting with your new manager and it's going well. Then they say, "Let's talk about the last day you'll work for me."

Startling, right? But I love this tip from speaker Charlene Li, author of the *New York Times* bestseller *Open Leadership*, who encourages managers to think about relationships with team members as *lifelong*. And since most of us work for different teams and companies over the course of our careers, it's wise to think this way from the get-go.

You might follow the "last day" question by saying, "I hope we work together for a long time, but I want our professional relationship to last even longer. I'd love to know what your goals are for the future, so I can help you get there." Li puts it this way:

> If I pretend that we'll work together for decades, that's not building integrity into the relationship. My role as a leader is to make sure my employees are growing and developing for whatever's next. If I can find their next role within the company, great. If not, I'll do everything I can to support them finding a position in which they'll thrive.

Li goes on to explain that most managers aren't having these conversations because they're afraid that talking openly about an employee's tenure at a company is disloyal. But, she argues, if we stop pretending and rethink the process, we can build relationships with our employees based on trust, integrity, honesty, and fairness.[1] Powerful, isn't it? Imagine how supported your team members will feel knowing you have the best interests of their full career in mind.

Map Out Their Journey—Start with Intentional Conversations

You don't need to be a mind reader to understand your team's career goals. Start by addressing it in your one-on-one conversations. Yes, it requires time and effort, but the return on investment (ROI) is huge. Ask questions like "What do you love most about your work?" "Where would you love to be in the next two to three years?" and "What's something you've always wanted to learn or try?" These questions invite deeper insights and help you understand what really drives them. And, bonus, people tend to feel pretty good reflecting on and envisioning these things!

Once you know their aspirations, get creative. Help them brainstorm growth opportunities that line up with their interests. It might involve a cross-department project, a mentorship with someone they admire, or even a stretch assignment that challenges them in new ways. Push them outside their comfort zones. But (and this is a big but) make sure they have the right support to succeed (think go-to person they can consult with questions, help to secure a budget, or air cover from you to protect time for the stretch opportunity).

Support Their Growth Even if It Means Letting Go

The tricky part of crafting growth journeys? Supporting your team members' development even if it means they'll eventually outgrow your team. I know I've felt a blow to my ego when a star team member transitioned to a new opportunity, but here's the truth: That's a total win. You've helped them achieve their potential, and that's what great leadership is all about. Low-ego, people-first leadership means you don't keep people around for your own gain (like that Star Wars collectible that's still in the original box!). You empower them to flourish, wherever that may lead.

Quick Wins to Start Building Their Growth Path

- Start with those one-on-ones. Understand their passions and goals.
- Collaborate on a development plan that includes training, mentorship, or new exposure or opportunities.
- Don't be afraid to suggest internal moves or stretch assignments outside of their current role.
- Provide regular feedback and celebrate progress, no matter how small.

There's a misconception that a leader's job is to hold onto their best people. The truth is, your job is to help them become the best version of themselves, whether that's on your team *or beyond it*. So become known as an investor—a people investor. After all, as a leader, you have the responsibility to nurture growth, not just for your benefit, but for theirs.

Tip 3: Have a Failure Party

In a work world that usually celebrates only success, let's change the way we think. If you want innovation, it's time to celebrate failure. Not the "sulk in silence" kind, but the "We learned something huge" kind. When failure is seen as a discovery, not a disaster, it seeds a culture where people feel free to experiment and grow.

Why Celebrate Failure?

I look at it like this: Failure isn't the end. It's a crucial part of growth. Just think about the last time you learned something significant. Chances are, it involved a few bumps. And when you take surviving those bumps a step further and share failure stories, you tell your team that mistakes aren't punishable; they're part of learning. Of course, this doesn't apply to a little "oops" (like the time Steve forgot to hit "Save" on a PowerPoint), but true setbacks? Those are moments for reflection, growth, and yes, celebration.

Get Real About Your Failures

Start with yourself. As a leader, be transparent about your setbacks, what you learned from them, and how they've shaped your leadership style. Trust me, nothing builds team rapport faster than a good laugh over shared mistakes. It sends a powerful message: *We're all in this together, and we're all learning.* You might share a story like this: "I once spent three days troubleshooting an issue that turned out to be a simple fix. It taught me to ask for help sooner. Here's what else I learned...." Your team will appreciate your openness, and they'll feel encouraged to share their own "oops" moments.

I'll demonstrate right now: Early in my career, I was so eager to please a client that I kept saying yes to every little extra request—until my team was drowning in work. I was too nervous to set limits late in the game for fear I'd look unaccommodating, and sure enough, it backfired. The client started expecting unlimited custom requests, and my team was frustrated, overworked, and looking to me for answers (*where was the sh!t umbrella?*). I had to own up to my mistake and reset client expectations, which wasn't fun, but it led to a new saying in our group: *Set limits on scope creep now, or you'll be setting 'em forever.*

Throw a Failure Party (Seriously)

Let's get to the fun part: the Failure Party. This shouldn't be a downcast event where everyone reads from a list of their mistakes. Instead, it's a low-pressure gathering where your team shares "failure stories" and the lessons that came from them. Bonus points if you bring snacks or a little bubbly.

The goal? To inject some humor and learning into the mix. The more lighthearted and fun you make this experience, the more your team will feel comfortable being open about their own failures in the future. I once had a client who got so into the concept, they brought "failure snacks" to their party—soft cheese spreads on "burnt toast" points to represent their cringeworthy moments. It became a pretty hilarious way to bond over the messes along the way.

Keep It Solution-Focused

When your team shares their "failure stories," keep the focus on learning. Ask questions like:

- "What would you do differently next time?"
- "What did you discover that you hadn't expected?"
- "How can we apply this lesson moving forward?"

You can even start tracking the lessons your team learns from failure and turn them into a "Lessons Learned" or "Failure Wins" board, which highlights the new insights gained from setbacks. This way, failure isn't just something that happened and is forgotten. It's also not cloaked in shame in a dark supply closet. It's something that contributes to the larger mission of growth, and your team can see the tangible value it brings.

Celebrate the Lessons, Not Just the Wins

A Failure Party reminds people in a non-subtle way that risk-taking is encouraged, innovation is embraced, and employees shouldn't be afraid to try new things. (*Aah, my shoulders are relaxing just writing that.*) When failure is no longer a dirty word, it opens the door for creative problem-solving and teamwork. Plus it helps build our bounce-back muscle of resilience—a major ingredient for long-term success.

Ultimately, by celebrating failure, you show your team that setbacks aren't something to be ashamed of. Every "oops" might just be an "aha!" in disguise.

Tip 4: Mentor More, Manage Less

The less experienced the manager, the more they tend to manage with a heavy dose of control: directing tasks, giving specific answers, and taking over if things become too much. It feels safe, right? You get to make all the decisions, and your team follows along. But here's the thing: When you manage more than you mentor, you create dependency. Your team might meet deadlines, but are they taking real ownership? Are they thinking creatively? Most importantly, are they motivated?

Mentorship, on the other hand, creates a space of collaboration. When you spend at least 50% of your time asking reflective questions, you not only develop critical thinking skills but you foster an empowered team that's ready to tackle the challenges that come their way.

The Power of Reflective Questions

Let's be real for a second: Nobody has the answers to everything. (And if they say they do, run!) That's why one powerful thing you can do as a mentor is prompt your team to think for themselves. I call this "Ask Three Before You Solve." So before you jump in with the solution, you get *them* to consider the situation first, by asking three questions.

So instead of saying, "This is how you should approach this task," try asking:

- "What's the most important thing you want to achieve here?"
- "Who do you think could be your biggest champion for this initiative?"
- "What obstacles do you anticipate, and how might you overcome them?"
- "How does this align with your long-term goals?"
- "What's the next step in this process, and how can we build on that?"

Asking these types of questions makes space for problem-solving and strategic thinking. And an awesome extra, it shows your team members autonomy and respect.

Nurture Growth Together

When you mentor, you send a loud message: *Your growth is just as important as your deliverables.* That's why it's important to connect people's current work to where they want to go in the future. Think of it as a two-way street: You're providing guidance, but they're providing you with insights about their strengths, motivations, and ambitions. You can ask:

- "How do you think this project could impact your long-term career path?"

- "What role do you want to play in shaping the future of this team?"

- "What skill would you most like to develop in the next six months, and how can we make that happen?"

These forward-looking questions help your team members focus on their own growth. And they can also start to align their goals with the broader mission or needs of the team or company. You empower them to become more than just workers; they become architects of their career advancement and future.

Lead by Example: Mentoring Through Transparency

Show, don't just tell. As a mentor, share your own lessons learned and the challenges you've overcome. And don't be surprised if your people start to open up and reflect more on their own growth. Remember, mentorship doesn't require you to have all the answers. Nor do you need to keep a "Pocket-Sized Book of Perfect Solutions" in a secret compartment. It's the human stuff of guiding your team, asking the right questions, and letting *them* discover their own solutions.

One mentor of mine, Sheila, generously shared a fumble that I think back on often. She was emphasizing the importance of language and words when we're trying to influence others. She explained to me before an important pitch she made to a new industry, she failed to refresh herself on the latest terminology. She ended up using outdated acronyms and terms, something that totally killed her credibility with the client (even if her proposal and ideas were smart). For a mentor, these "ick" moments and cautionary tales mean everything to your mentees. They impart the core lesson but also show that even seasoned professionals make mistakes—and recover from them. I still think back on this and use it to check myself before working with a new client or in a rapidly changing industry!

Be the Mentor, Not the Manager

Free yourself from old ideas of command and control leadership. No more temptations to give the "right" answer; instead, you pause. And you ask your people questions that prompt reflection, creativity, and growth. In the end, you'll cultivate a more innovative, motivated, and forward-thinking team—one that's capable of far more than you could ever manage.

Tip 5: Stoke Individual Strengths

Your team's talent is like the ultimate potluck: Every person brings something different to the table. When you tap into what makes each person shine, the mood shifts. Things feel less mandated and forced. People feel more confident and take more initiative. Think about it: When was the last time you felt truly valued for something specific you brought to the table? Pretty great, right? That's the feeling you want for your team members.

The Power of Specific Appreciation

Here's the deal: Generic praise like "Great job!" or "You're awesome!" sounds nice on the surface, but it's too vague to mean anything. If you want to fuel individual strengths, get specific. Name what they did and why it made a difference. For example, "I loved how you handled the client's out-of-scope requests in the meeting. You accommodated their need but communicated clear boundaries on delivery dates. You modeled how to be assertive." This type of recognition makes people feel seen, heard, and valued. And think about how the person now has a clear picture of the positive behavior, so they can repeat it in the future.

Create a Culture of Strengths, Not Just Weaknesses

In a lot of workplaces, the focus is often on fixing weaknesses. I still remember doing focus groups at an investment bank where I asked, "What's one phrase that describes the attitude toward building strengths and working on weaknesses here?" A woman said matter-of-factly, "We don't suffer fools lightly. Strengths are assumed; weaknesses are the only things deemed worthy of discussion." Oof! Talk about a culture that makes you want to hide, downplay, or ignore weaknesses—not to mention one that's draining and demotivating. Instead, be the leader that legitimizes and leans into your team's strengths. Encourage people to talk about what they excel at and give them opportunities to test those abilities. Maybe Sarah has a knack for simplifying complex processes. Or perhaps Neil has an eye for design that could elevate your next project. Embolden them to own their strengths and take the lead where their skills really shine.

Let People Lead from Their Strengths

Put people in the arenas where their natural talents ignite. If someone is amazing at managing logistics, put them in charge of an upcoming project. If someone thrives in brainstorming sessions, make sure they have a voice when new ideas are being formed.

To help your team reflect on their unique talents, ask them questions like:

- What tasks or projects do you feel most energized by? Why do you think that is?
- What's something you've tackled recently that made you feel confident in your abilities?
- What strengths do you believe you bring to the team that set you apart from others?

- How can you use your strengths to help others on the team or to solve problems we're currently facing?

- Is there a new challenge or project you'd like to take on that aligns with your strengths? What would that look like?

These questions? They're little sparks, nudging your people to think proactively about how they can multiply their strengths by three. And that's no small thing!

Cultivate a Culture of Strengths

Champion the kind of leadership that recognizes everyone's contribution, whether it's the analytical thinker, the creative fire-starter, or the person who always gets the team out of a tech jam.

Cultivate a team where individuality isn't just tolerated, it's celebrated. They'll be motivated to bring their best work every single day. Who wouldn't be fired up?

Tip 6: Progress Over Perfection

My kryptonite has always been perfectionism. I've definitely sat in never-ending loops of trying to make something "perfect": the endless tweaking, the overthinking, the "Wait, wait, let me just add one more thing" desperation. (Deep breaths—I'm over it now … mostly.) Maybe you've been there?

One time, working on a client report, I missed the actual deadline. I was so caught up in refining indents and little word-choice decisions that I lost sight of the bigger picture—getting the thing done! The kicker? No one would have noticed the tiny improvements I obsessed over. That moment taught me an uncomfortable but necessary lesson: Done is better than perfect, and sometimes the best thing you can do is hit send and move on. I can now see that perfectionism isn't just unnecessary; it's counterproductive.

What Really Matters: Impact Over Immaculate

When you shift your focus from perfect outcomes to meaningful impact, everything changes. Forward movement—endeavoring and iterating, gives you direction, clarity, and energy. Whereas striving for perfect? It just drains your enthusiasm and sets an out-of-reach bar. Perfection is like a fancy, delicious-looking cake behind glass, slowly going stale while you admire it—forever preserved and uneaten! But observing impact, noticing little gains in progress? That's the yummy, wholesome meal—the fortifier you can access—that fuels you and keeps you going.

When "Good Enough" Leads to Great

Excellence means giving your best effort while accepting that things won't always go perfectly. You're showing up with intention, doing the work with care, and being open to learning from the inevitable missteps along the way.

To cascade this mindset in your team, communicate that your standard is reaching for excellence, progress, and learning. For example, you might say:

- "Let's focus on delivering a high-quality result and refine it along the way."
- "What's most important here is making progress, even if it's not perfectly airtight."
- "We can always iterate and improve this after we get a first draft in place."
- "The goal here is to give an excellent presentation, not to make it flawless."
- "Let's prioritize making an impact over getting every detail perfect."

The message here is focused on continuous improvement, action, and results—*to a healthy degree.*

Lead Without the Pressure Cooker

So how do you lead your team in this shift? Start by modeling it yourself. Let your team see that sometimes you have to do your best with limited resources or partial information. Talk about how you'll adjust your approach and what you learned from the experience. Say that you're trying for a very good end result, trusting that you can improve it and make progress on it over time. If you see someone else struggling with perfectionism, offer support, as in "I see you putting a lot into this. From what I've seen, it's strong and ready for the next step. This is a learning process, and getting it out there will allow us to get feedback and refine it further."

One study in the journal *Personality and Individual Differences* shows this kind of offer of help from peers actually reduces the stress of perfectionism and increases the likelihood of innovation.[2] When you create a culture where imperfection is viewed as an opportunity for growth, that's a sweet spot. Your team will feel encouraged to take calculated risks and pursue projects with passion, not fear.

Allow Room for Growth

Remind your team that excellence doesn't mean flawless execution. Perfection is exhausting and frankly nonexistent, and the pursuit of it can sap the joy out of work. When you shift the focus from perfect results to meaningful progress, people stop walking on eggshells and start thinking bigger. That's when real creativity shows up and your team actually has the energy to build, solve, and try again. So be real. Give people permission to be human. *Be perfectly imperfect.*

Tip 7: Invest in Their Skills

I'll never forget when my former boss gave our entire consulting team a new mandate. *It made me sweat.* We were required to publish three to four articles a year and present at just as many conferences! *Whoa.* I was equal parts freaked out and excited.

Looking back, being lovingly "shoved" into that skill-building opportunity is what set me on my path as a writer and speaker—two outlets that I discovered I absolutely love. I'm still thankful for that boss! If you want to show you're committed to *your* people's long-term success, provide real opportunities to grow (not just more work with a fancier title). This isn't just a nice-to-have for your team; it's going to help them stay competitive and engaged.

Upskilling Is a Necessity, Not a Luxury

Right now, skills can become outdated faster than … skinny jeans—one day they're in, the next day they're collecting dust in the back of your closet. Hey, don't look at me; I don't make the fashion rules. Investing in your team's development means regularly keeping your eyes and ears open for ways they can keep their skills fresh. Think about it: If for some (totally benign) reason you had to quit tomorrow, wouldn't you want to know your people were equipped to tackle the challenges around the corner? Well, you encouraging them to get involved with formal training, conferences, or more casual skill-building activities will help keep learning front and center, give them agility, and build great reflexes for the unexpected.

Conferences: Learning, Networking, and Inspiration

Conferences are a fantastic way to expose your team to new ideas, trends, and networking opportunities. Consider sending them to industry events, like TEDx or regional leadership summits as a participant. And if it's a match, nominate them to speak on a panel or represent your organization. These experiences can broaden their horizons and connect them with relevant other professionals. And, powerfully, they can take those exposure opportunities with them wherever they go, for the rest of their lives.

Formal Training: Filling Knowledge Gaps

If you fight for anything for your team, the professional development budget should be among the top three causes. Formal training, like certifications or specialized courses, translates to better pay in many cases for your employees. The focus might be project management workshops or leadership development programs; either way, you're setting them up to be better equipped to thrive. And the bonus? This is one less thing you have to do.

Remind your team that learning doesn't stop at formal courses. Ask them to pursue continuing education through platforms like Coursera, Udemy, or LinkedIn Learning. These options are flexible and cost-effective and put employees in control. They can choose topics that boost skills on a set learning path, or take a one-off course. And since many of these online courses are self-paced, your employees can maintain their day-to-day responsibilities. The point is to create a culture that values ongoing learning, micro or macro!

Regional Associations: Building Community and Leadership

Regional associations are another great resource for skill development. Local chapters of professional organizations often offer workshops, webinars, and events that can help team members grow in their field. But why not encourage your people to step into a leadership role (like treasurer, chairperson, or advocacy lead) and shape the discourse? The chance to network with others in their industry, make calls and decisions, and (obviously) forge connections can be priceless.

Grow as You Go

There's the development you need to sign up for. Then there's the everyday, on-the-job opportunities that help your team grow. Give them challenging projects, ask them to give a lunch-and-learn on an area they researched, or nominate them to deliver the presentation. Showing that you give a hoot about their development is crucial. That's true whether it's nudging them to expand their horizons or telling them about a great stretch opportunity.

Eight in ten workers say learning enhances their sense of purpose at work.[3] When you prioritize learning, you're building commitment, innovation, and a team that's ready to tackle whatever comes next. Invest in your people like they're your greatest resource. Their development is the foundation of your next big win.

Tip 8: Flexibility Fuels Productivity

Expecting people to conform to the staid nine-to-five grind isn't leadership—it's babysitting in business casual. In today's workplace, you can't be the kind of leader who's tallying who got here first today or who ducked out early last Thursday. It's about delivering results.

Rethink What "Work Hours" Mean

Give your team the freedom to work when and where they're most focused. Early birds can tackle complex tasks at dawn, while your night owls can dive in after sunset. Flexibility helps people align their work schedules and rhythms with their peak performance hours. That's a win for both employees and the business.

Example in action: Allow team members to adjust their hours individually, like logging in early to finish by midafternoon or starting later after school drop-off. Then trust them to manage their time. To be clear, this isn't a free pass to disappear into the abyss of unread Slack messages. But it is a commitment that you'll focus on outcomes, not clock-watching.

Flexibility Builds Trust (and Loyalty)

Micromanaging every hour kills morale faster than a back-to-back meeting marathon. Flexibility, though, shows you trust your team to manage their responsibilities without hovering. It also sends a powerful message: "I see you as a capable adult, not a productivity robot."

Example in action: Try a "core hours" policy where everyone is online for key collaborative hours, but the rest is flexible. This helps balance structure with freedom.

Real Life Happens—Plan for It

If I've learned anything as a working mom of twins (who also cares for an elderly mom), it's that life doesn't follow office hours. From surprise school closures to impromptu appointments and health scares, personal responsibilities pop up. Flexible leaders understand this (they even anticipate it!) and create a culture where asking for schedule adjustments isn't taboo—it's expected.

Example in action: Allow employees to block time for personal obligations. One manager I coached shared a team calendar labeled "Life Happens" where team members could note when they were out for personal reasons, no awkward explanations required.

The Remote Work Reality Check

Flexibility is certainly about *where* people can work. It's also about *how*. Please, don't be the manager who defines working remotely as being chained to a desk at home and whose skepticism meter goes off the charts when people have autonomy. Encourage employees to work from places that spark creativity—a quiet cafe, a library, or even a park bench.

Example in action: Consider shaking things up with a "Work from Anywhere" week where team members are encouraged to switch up their environments. This "little" invitation can seismically boost both productivity and creativity. Think of the message: Your best work matters, and I trust you to define how that happens (regardless of zip code!).

Flexibility as a Retention Superpower

Employees today value flexibility as much as salary (sometimes more). Offering it isn't a frill; it's a retention strategy. So set clear goals, deadlines, and expectations, then get out of the way. If you're not offering flexibility, your competitors will—and your talent will notice.

Example in action: Highlight your flexible work policies in job listings and interviews. Show prospective hires that you *live flexibility*, you don't just preach it.

The Future Is Flexible

Flexibility is the ultimate productivity and morale booster and a key ingredient in fostering trust, loyalty, and well-being. Spark a "Great Rethink" in your workplace about traditional work hours, starting with allowing your team to work when and where they're most effective. That way, life's unpredictable moments won't derail productivity or more broadly, someone's chances of advancement. Embrace the freedom to focus on what truly matters: outcomes. Flexibility is here to stay.

Tip 9: Paint the Future Together: Shared Vision, Individual Roles

You've instilled purpose. You've illuminated the bigger Why. Now, to *really* underscore meaningful work, you need to go beyond simply showing people the sketch of what's next. You need to help them trace their own connection to it, so that everyone understands and feels connected to *their impact* in the unfolding future. This final piece of the meaning puzzle makes the future a collaborative creation, where every individual sees their brushstroke on the evolving canvas.

Co-create the Vision: Involve Them in Crafting What's Ahead

If you want your team to truly own the future, turn them into "future scouts." Think of it like equipping them with little spyglasses! Focus their energy on dissecting the evolving landscape by hosting "trend-spotting" sessions to study what's happening *outside* your four walls. These ideas can help you get started:

- **Deep dive January: competitor innovation** A different team analyzes a competitor's recent bold move and discusses its potential implications for your strategy.

- **Customer whisperers: spot evolving needs** Task individuals with engaging (through surveys, social listening, or even informal conversations) with current customers to identify unmet needs.

- **Tech radar: identify game changers** Assign team members to track specific technological advancements (AI, blockchain, etc.) and present on their potential disruptive or enabling power.

- **Industry shifts: navigate regulatory/societal tides** Ask the group to research and share regulatory changes, evolving societal values, and their potential impact on your market and operations.

During these sessions, you're ideating how your company can proactively adapt, capitalize, or even disrupt based on these external forces. Document these insights! They're the raw materials for your shared vision.

Chart Their Footprint: Connect Current Tasks to Future Goals

Once a collaborative vision solidifies, articulate how each individual's current responsibilities directly contribute to achieving future aspirations. End a meeting by "connecting the dots" where you use examples like:

- "Sarah, your work on improving customer onboarding today directly impacts our goal of increasing customer retention by 15% next year."
- "Mark, the scalability improvements you're implementing now are foundational for our expansion into new markets in the following quarter."
- "The marketing campaigns you're developing, Lisa, are building the brand awareness needed for our Q4 product launch."

Be specific. Show the direct cause-and-effect relationship between their daily tasks and long-term success.

Tell the "Then and Now" Story

Human brains are wired for stories. So paint a compelling picture of your group's evolution. Use "The Hero's Journey" or another framework to tell your story—or create a short "day in the life" scenario depicting your work's future impact on customers or communities. Other ideas include:

- Create a visual roadmap of your group's path, goals, milestones, and even some of the "inclement weather" you faced.

- Share short videos showcasing prototypes or early successes related to future initiatives.

- During team meetings, dedicate a few minutes to tell a "Then and Now" story—where your group was, steps taken (including *their* contributions), and where it's heading.

Regular Vision Refresh: Keep the Future Top of Mind

The future—*surprise, surprise!*—needs to be a recurring conversation. Regularly revisit your vision. Connect new wins back to it. Make it hard to forget about: Integrate the future vision into your communications (newsletters, internal updates) and put up visual reminders of the future vision in team workspaces like a "future timeline" wall, infographic, or future state mockups (you'll find little visual nudges can work wonders). And, certainly, encourage open dialogue and feedback on the evolving vision. Are there any roadblocks? New opportunities? That keeps things dynamic and relevant.

See how this creates a future that's more "collaborative project" than corporate decree? You're igniting a sense of collective purpose, where every team member understands their vital role in building something significant—together. This isn't just a future we imagine; it's a future we'll craft, stroke by collaborative stroke.

5 Handling the Hard Stuff with Heart

Here's a truth about leadership we don't always say out loud—it's not all team victories, poise under pressure, and being seen as the go-to. Sometimes it's stepping into a room knowing you're about to have a conversation no one wants to have. It's the stuff that makes your palms sweat, your heart race, and your stomach churn—a difficult decision, that one team member who's been dropping the ball consistently despite your previous conversations, a missed critical deadline. This chapter is your toolkit for those moments.

Tough conversations aren't anyone's favorite part of the job, but they're often where real leadership shows up. This chapter will help you navigate those moments with clarity, calm, and a little more confidence. Ignoring conflicts and challenging dynamics only breeds confusion, resentment ... and those awkward passive-aggressive emails and weird eyerolls no one likes. Conflict doesn't disappear on its own. If you think it has, that means it's creeping below like a sea monster. *Yikes!* Instead, let's talk about handling it with a blend of compassion and directness. Because when you approach conflict with a people-first mindset, you go beyond resolving issues; you're stacking the bricks for a rock-solid foundation of trust and respect.

We'll dive into how to walk *toward* these conversations with empathy, keeping your cool while delivering the kind of feedback that sticks (without sticking it to the person). That means for all leaders, we need to learn to ride the wave of discomfort, knowing it's survivable and a sign that growth is happening. By tackling the tough stuff, you're modeling the kind of courage and resilience you want your team to embrace. So gear up. The real magic happens when you consistently confront challenges not just with a plan but with courage, purpose, and your humanity intact.

Tip 1: Have the Hard Conversations Now, Not Later

When a problem arises in your team, the easiest response might be to push it aside, hoping it resolves itself. Lord knows I've been in that position, particularly when the person I managed—and needed to confront—was also someone I considered a friend. *No one* loves stepping into a potentially awkward or confrontational discussion.

But here's how I think of these conversations: It's a bit like molding a clay pot. There's a crucial window in ceramics to shape, refine, and fix something, but wait too long and the clay hardens, the glaze is applied, and once it's been through the kiln, your chance to fix things in a timely way is gone! In a similar sense, addressing issues early allows for adjustments while there's still flexibility. It helps you prevent problems from solidifying into bigger, tougher challenges.

The Myth of Perfect Timing

One of the biggest traps leaders fall into is waiting for the "just right" time to address an issue. Heads-up: There is no perfect time; there's only the time you intentionally create (and if you're waiting for all the different stars to align, you might be waiting for a while)! Life is busy and messy, projects overlap, and stress levels ebb and flow. Banking on a calm or ideal moment means waiting ... forever. Instead, prioritize the conversation. It doesn't have to be an elaborate meeting. Sometimes a simple, honest chat can make all the difference.

The Power of Now

Maybe it's a team member who's consistently missed deadlines or someone who "quiet quit" long ago—*and kind of loudly*. These situations don't improve on their own; they create a ripple effect of confusion and resentment, and sour team morale. But when you deal with challenges as they arise, you're communicating: *We don't run from problems here. We face them, fix them, and grow from them.* That's powerful. It's proactive. It builds trust and sets a precedent for open communication. It also demonstrates that you're a leader who values transparency and growth, not looking the other way.

How to Approach the Conversation

It helps to kick things off by introducing the conversation focus. You might begin with "I wanted us to have the chance to discuss X today," or "I'd like to share some observations with you about ABC." This sets the tone for a productive chat where you're addressing a specific issue, not launching an interrogation. You can also address (and adapt) these elements:

1. **Start with empathy.** Acknowledge the other person's perspective. "I've noticed some things that might be affecting your work, and I want to understand your side."

2. **Be clear and direct.** State the issue without ambiguity or sugarcoating. "I've observed that deadlines have been slipping, and it's causing delays in the team's overall progress. Can we talk about what's going on and how we can fix it?"

3. **Focus on solutions.** Frame the discussion around resolving, not assigning blame. "I'm more interested in figuring out what we can

do to get back on track than detailing all that went wrong. Let's talk about how we can address this moving forward."

4. **Follow up.** Reinforce that you're here and plan to reconnect/reassess. "I'm going to check in with you next week to see how things are going. Let me know if you need any support along the way. I'm here to help."

Don't Let the Clay Harden

Remember, the longer you wait, the harder it is to make meaningful changes. There's a critical period where intervention can shape the outcome. Act while the problem is still malleable. Waiting might feel easier in the moment, but it often leads to missed opportunities for growth and improvement. If not now, then when?

Tip 2: Hard-Hitting Feedback, but Make It Kind

I'll never forget watching a leadership speaker deliver a riveting keynote to 3,000 people. He was charismatic, commanding the stage in a black T-shirt and jeans, completely captivating the audience. But there it was—a big, white price tag sticking out of the back of his shirt, dangling on a hangtag. Somehow, through all the tech checks and handlers, no one told him. Awkward, right? Everyone saw it, but no one overcame their hesitation to say something. The same goes for giving your team honest feedback: Skip over it, and it's like the flashing neon sign everyone's pretending not to see.

Make It Thoughtful

If you want to be known as the kind of leader who demonstrates respect for the individual and the team, the key is to keep it truthful and constructive. To guide you in delivering feedback thoughtfully, remember the acronym KIND:

- **K**eep it specific
- **I**nquire with empathy
- **N**eutralize blame
- **D**irect toward solutions

Keep It Specific Vague feedback helps no one. Focus on specific behaviors rather than making general or personal remarks. For example, instead of saying, "You're always late," try "I noticed you were late to the last three meetings, which affected the team's progress." This approach helps the recipient understand the exact issue and its impact.

Inquire with Empathy Before jumping to conclusions, ask questions to understand the situation. After all, a feedback conversation is more productive when it feels like a dialogue, not a lecture. For example, "Is there something that's been preventing you from meeting deadlines?" shows concern and opens the door for a constructive conversation.

Neutralize Blame Focus your language on actions and outcomes rather than personal attributes. Go out of your way not to use words that feel accusatory. For instance, "Your report was missing key data points, which delayed our project," is better than "You messed up the report." This keeps the feedback professional and objective.

Direct Toward Solutions Feedback should be future-focused. After identifying the issue, you can shift to discussing how it can be resolved. Ask, "What steps can we take to make sure this doesn't happen again?" or "How can I support you to meet deadlines?" This "one team" approach encourages growth and accountability.

Keep the Dialogue Open

Feedback is rarely a one-time event; it's part of an ongoing conversation. Plus, it's your chance to offer continued support, make adjustments, and maybe, just maybe, avoid that disappointing "I'm not sure where we went wrong" moment down the road. Keep it flowing, and your team will keep rising.

Timing Is Key

Find a moment soon after the event when emotions have settled but the details are still fresh. Prompt, timely feedback shows you prioritize honesty and transparency. That balance—being timely without being rushed—makes all the difference. And remember Tip 8 from Chapter 1: "Praise Publicly, Coach Privately." Feedback lands best when it's given with care and a li'l dose of consideration.

Lead with Compassion

Keeping reminding yourself to see feedback not as something critical or harsh, but as straightforward information-sharing. When you approach it with care and clarity, it feels less like a punishment and more like a chance to grow. So next time you notice a metaphorical price tag sticking out, say something—just do it with empathy!

Tip 3: Let Go of the "Nice Boss" Complex

Growing up, my family had a way of tiptoeing around tough conversations. If there was a problem or fight, it often got swept under the rug, or we danced around it with vague hints and hopeful smiles. Maybe you can relate? Whether or not you come from a background like mine, you might find yourself leaning toward a more indirect approach when things get uncomfortable. But in leadership, prioritizing harmony at all costs is aiming for the wrong target. Same with trying to be the eternal good gal/guy. You risk sidestepping tough decisions, which can undermine trust and credibility. As a leader, the assignment is clear: say it directly, out loud, and with purpose ('cuz tiptoeing will never do).

Transparency Over Sugarcoating

Let's say you have to give one of your top reports some tough news that the company is putting the brakes on their passion project. The temptation to sugarcoat or soften the message is real. But transparency is precisely what the person needs! Instead of diluting the truth, offer a full, honest picture, including context if relevant. Transparency builds trust and sets clear expectations, even when the news isn't what people want to hear.

Wes Kao, a tech founder and executive coach, calls this "emotional signposting," and it's powerful. She explains:

> As humans, we like knowing the "right" reaction to a piece of news. It's jarring when you expect to be emotionally led in one direction, but the message goes in a different direction. It's unsettling, confusing, and adds cognitive load.
>
> Emotional signposting is giving your audience clues about whether a piece of information is positive, negative, or neutral. It's tacitly suggesting how your audience should interpret what you just told them.[1]

Keeping with our example, you could say, "I have a disappointing update about your project. I know how much it means to you, and I want to be transparent. Due to new priorities, the company decided to pull your budget and allocate the resources elsewhere. Let's talk about what this means for you and how we can adjust together." Contrast this with a more indirect, sugarcoated approach: "The project's just not a fit anymore, but don't worry, we'll find something else for you." The latter is vague and dismissive, which leaves the employee confused and undervalued. So be upfront! Say the unvarnished truth, offer support, and show your respect for their dedication and effort. *That's* what builds trust.

The Power of Directness

If they're unsure, that's on you. So keep it clear and simple. Because guess what happens in the absence of clear information? You create a vacuum that gets filled with assumptions and anxiety. Being direct allows your team to understand expectations and act accordingly.

Imagine you need to tell a valued team member they won't be leading an upcoming high-profile project. A not-great approach is "We've decided to go in a different direction, but don't worry, you'll have other opportunities." This vague reassurance skirts the real issue and mucks up the real Why.

Instead, a more direct approach is "We've decided to assign the project to someone else because we need a different set of skills for our particular challenge of XYZ." Then follow up with these key points:

Aim for Considerate, Not Coddling

- Acknowledge their effort: "I appreciate the hard work you've put into this."
- Offer reassurance: "This doesn't reflect on your overall performance but is about finding the right fit for this specific task."

Open the Door for Dialogue

- Encourage input: "How are you feeling about this?"
- Invite their perspective: "Do you have any thoughts on how we can move forward?"

When you communicate honestly and simply, even tough calls feel more respectful than harsh.

Ditch the "Nice Boss" Label for "Respected Leader"

A respected leader pursues integrity and truth like a dog chasing a squirrel: relentlessly and with purpose! It's not about being everyone's friend; it's about being the one who tells it straight, offers support, and makes the tough calls. Letting go of the "Nice Boss" complex means stepping into a leadership style that's genuine, grounded, and refreshingly human.

Tip 4: Top of Form

Empathy Isn't Endless Patience

Ah, empathy . . . the admiration-worthy quality that helps you connect with your team and shows you care. It's both needed and rare. But you know what empathy *isn't*? Endless patience. Like the kind where you endure half-hearted tries or limp excuses. That's not empathy. It's letting people walk all over you.

You know what I mean, right? That one team member who "didn't see" the requests or the other who's "really working on that project." There's no need to suffer foolishness. It's time for you as a leader to shift from "I'll let this slide" to "Let's fix this." What people need isn't avoidant tolerance, but a leader who challenges them and holds them accountable.

Support Your Team, But Hold 'Em Accountable

Accountability is where the stakes get real. It's where the truth comes out. And I'm not making a light suggestion. It's a nonnegotiable part of leadership. After all, you can't lead with *only empathy*—you've got to balance it with clear expectations and follow-through. If not, you risk enabling your team to languish or to become straight-up complacent. You can support your team, of course, but you also need to make sure they're delivering what they promised.

Call People in, Not Out

Ever discovered a mistake where your first instinct was to yell, *"How did this get so screwed up? Who did this?!"* Totally fair. But let's take a beat before we go full courtroom drama with "Exhibit A: your massive flop!" Calling someone out feels like putting them on trial: "You messed up. Here's the evidence. Now, suffer the consequences." *No thanks!* Instead, try calling them *in*. You're inviting them into a conversation where they can take responsibility and work with you to find a solution. No shame, just accountability. For example, instead of saying, "You're not doing your job," try "I've noticed your work recently hasn't been at the level we need. Let's talk about what's been going on and how we can get back on track." See the difference? You're solving the issue together, not just blaming. That's a way more productive approach.

Compassionate and Firm: The Best of Both Worlds

Think about a great sports coach. They cheer the team on when they're excelling or trying hard, but they're also the one calling them out when they skip the fundamentals. Not just that, but it's normal for a coach to openly address the role an individual played in an outcome.

So how do you shape a coaching environment where everyone takes responsibility for their actions and outcomes? It starts with setting clear expectations and communicating in a way that strikes a balance between leadership and empathy. That might sound like:

- "I know you've got it in you, but this isn't where we need to be. Let's talk about how we can close the gap."
- "This is where I need you to step up. I believe you can do it but it's on you to follow through."
- "I know things have been tough lately, but that doesn't change the expectations. Let's brainstorm how to get back on track."
- "We've hit a roadblock and I can't let this slide. What can we do to get things moving again?"
- "I'm not seeing the effort we discussed and that needs to change. What's going on, and how can I help?"

You're Not a Patience ATM Machine

Empathy and accountability go hand-in-hand, but let's not confuse empathy with inaction. You do not need to be patient to a fault. Right now is the time to show you care enough to call out behavior when it's not up to standard. Show your team that you have their back, but you also expect results. That's the leadership formula that works.

Tip 5: Attack the Problem, Not the Person

My coaching client Brian was leading a high-stakes project at his company. Everything seemed on track until an unexpected team error—an overlooked step in the software deployment process derailed a crucial phase. Tensions were high, and in the heat of the moment, Brian gathered his team for a meeting. Instead of pointing fingers, he started the discussion with a simple question: "Can we walk through what happened?"

The room, initially tense, began to relax as one by one, team members volunteered their perspectives. Together, they identified the gap in the process that had led to the mistake. By focusing on the issue rather than blaming or shaming an individual, Brian not only figured out a path forward but also strengthened the team's trust and collaboration. For someone who had been working on managing his reactivity in the moment, this was a certified breakthrough! His approach turned a potentially divisive moment into an opportunity for growth.

So how do you shape an environment where everyone takes responsibility for their actions and outcomes? Let's break it down.

Create a Culture of Curiosity, Not Blame

In moments of stress or failure, there's definitely an urge to assign blame. But as Brian learned, this doesn't solve anything; it only alienates your team. So shift from a mindset of blame to one of curiosity. Ask open-ended questions to uncover what went wrong without pointing fingers:

- "What do you think caused the delay?"
- "How can we improve our process to find a way forward and avoid this in the future?"

These questions show you're interested in understanding and improving the situation, not attributing guilt. They open the door for less defensive dialogue and more collaborative problem-solving.

Focus on Solutions, Not Personalities

When a project goes sideways, you job is to steer the focus back to solutions. Try to approach a new issue as a team challenge, not an individual failing. Remember, your goal is to fix the process, not criticize the person.

Try phrases like:

- "What steps can we take to get back on track?"
- "Let's explore different solutions together."

Here, you're keeping the team united and motivated to find a resolution, *not* dividing them into the accused and the accusers.

Tackle the Issue, Not the Character

Last time I checked, assuming the worst doesn't help anyone. Instead, you can bring a little more balance by sticking to the facts.

Instead of saying, "You're always interrupting others in meetings," try "I noticed you interrupted Linda three different times in today's meeting. Can we talk about this?" This keeps the conversation focused on the situation and makes it easier to address without defensiveness. You can also try phrases like:

- "I understand the conversation was getting heated. How can we ensure this doesn't happen again?"
- "Let's get clear on how we can make space for everyone to share their thoughts without interruptions."

You're building trust and showing your team that while you care about them as individuals, you also expect them to rise to the challenge.

It's About Fixing, Not Faulting

When you target issues—not individuals, your tough conversations are more likely to lead to real solutions, where people feel safe acknowledging their role in what went sideways. Do that and you'll encourage a mindset of improvement. And you might just turn some of those fails and fumbles into ripe opportunities for growth.

Tip 6: Teach Your Employees to Self-Promote

Yuck. That's the reaction of many professionals I've trained on the topic of self-promotion.

But think about it. You've got hard-working, talented people who are giving so much to contribute to the team, yet when it comes to sharing their achievements, plenty of them freeze. It can feel like walking into a room, standing on a chair, and shouting their wins to a crowd of indifferent colleagues. No wonder it feels cringeworthy, right?

But say it with me: Self-promotion isn't bragging. Reduce it and you see that it's simply about sharing relevant information: wins and learnings, big and small, that make a difference for the team and the organization. And as a leader, you've got to teach your employees how to do this comfortably and confidently. Because unless you're a professional rapper or boxer, there's no hype person coming to do it for you,

Normalize Self-Promotion

If you're not actively encouraging your team to share their accomplishments, you're missing out. Why? Because you're not just a leader; you're also a facilitator of growth and opportunity. When your employees are open about their contributions, you stay informed, and your leaders (yes, those folks who don't often hear the good stuff) can get an ongoing feed of positive updates from you. Win-win, right?

You're also setting the stage for a culture of transparency and mutual respect. Imagine a workplace where no one is holding back or waiting for someone else to recognize their work. That's a team of motivated, confident individuals—of advocates!

Teach, Don't Just Tell

If you want your team to improve at self-promotion, here are some ways to show them how.

- **Set the example.** As a leader, say what *you're* proud of. Show your employees that it's normal and valuable to share progress. For example, "I'm proud of handling what was a tough client call last week. It was a challenge, but it turned into a great opportunity for us." Lead by example so they feel comfortable following suit.

- **Create a safe space.** This doesn't mean you need to hold a "Let's Talk Nonstop About Our Achievements" meeting every week (although, hey, that might be fun!). What it does mean is that it pays for you to foster an environment where self-promotion feels like a natural part of the conversation. You can offer prompts in meetings like "What's something you're proud of lately?"

- **Encourage the "micro-wins."** Not every celebration-worthy moment has to be a massive project completion. Encourage your team to talk about the little victories, solving a problem, upleveling a new skill, or getting positive feedback from a client. Aren't these the little things that get each of us through the day?! You can highlight little contributions by saying, "Tell us about a win this week, even a little one."

Share the Formula

Beyond incorporating these techniques into your own leadership arsenal, I encourage you to coach your employees to learn to self-promote outside the bounds of your department—not in the obnoxious way, but in an information- and resource-sharing way. Here are some simple ways they can share a win:

- **Set the context.** Frame the accomplishment: "I saw that our workflow on X was slowing us down, so I tested a new system to streamline the process."

- **Be specific.** Actions you took: "I implemented the new system, which cut our processing time by 30%. That's allowing us to handle more projects."

- **Highlight the impact.** Connect the result to the bigger picture: "This not only improved our efficiency but also helped us meet deadlines faster, boosting client satisfaction."

- **Share a relevant takeaway.** "I worked on a problem very similar to this and one best practice we took away was X. I think it applies here."

Spread the Wealth

Even though we know self-promotion isn't bragging, it can still be tough to start doing it, especially if you were raised to be humble or deflect pride. But here's some encouragement: Research from George Mason University found that self-promotion isn't harmful and *doesn't reduce likability* when it's combined with promoting others. We can hype ourselves up and confidently give airtime to our wins, as long as we *also* give credit and hype others up too. Combining these is called dual promotion, and it helps us be perceived as both competent and warm.[2]

So fear not. Whether you're a comfortable self-promoter or a table-diver, you can always lean on the power of social celebration, or "dual promotion." Want to highlight a recent win? Share your achievement while naming those who helped. I dare anyone to accuse you of "bragging" after that!

Shift the Mindset

Self-promotion isn't bragging, it's transparency. It's sharing valuable information. Maybe most important, it's a learning exchange. When done right, it builds a culture of openness, acknowledgment, and confidence. Don't wait—pass it on!

Tip 7: Redirect Praise, Absorb Criticism

It's easy to get caught up in praise. (I know that any author who's read a glowing Amazon review of their book would agree!) Taking in those serotonin-boosting accolades about a successful project or praise from a client can feel like the loveliest warm sunray. But here's the real deal: The most admiration-worthy leaders actually deflect praise *and* absorb criticism. Sounds counterintuitive, right? But it's a true sign of humility, respect, and emotional intelligence.

I'm asking you to be the kind of leader who shields your team from unnecessary blame and shares credit where it's due: with them.

Take the Heat, Then Turn Down the Temperature

When your team messes up, you have a choice: Heap on the accusations (like we established earlier in this chapter) or protect them from the fallout. In the first scenario, leaders might feel pressured to point fingers and say, "How *could* you have ... ?" Well guess what? That approach fosters fear, distrust, and a lack of accountability. Remember, one of your most defining moves is to act as the "sh!t umbrella," buffering your team from unnecessary blame.

So even if the issue occurred two levels down, own the mistake and be ready to address it. You might communicate that upward, saying, "We didn't hit the mark, and I'll take full responsibility for that," while encouraging your team to work together to figure out the solution. The simple act of absorbing the blame shows that you're willing to protect your people and shoulder the weight of leadership. And your team will respect you for it.

Redirect Praise to Your Team

Now, on the flip side, let's talk about redirecting praise. When your team does something amazing like solving a complex issue, landing a new client, or meeting a goal ahead of schedule, redirect the glory. Don't be the hero in this story. Highlight the individuals or the team who made a difference: "I'm blown away by the hard work of Daniella and Mark who really amazed us with their presentation. Daniella led the engaging delivery and Mark made sure the content was just right for the client."

In moments like this, your role as a leader is to play the part of the cheerleader (not star of the show). Do that, and you'll demonstrate in action that your leadership is about *their growth, not your ego.* And bonus: when praise is deflected properly, it makes your team more likely to take risks and collaborate openly, ready to contribute their best. *Pretty nice!*

Lead with Humility, Reap the Rewards

If you've been looking for ways to make your people feel safe, valued, and empowered to perform at their best, try the moves I've laid out here. The next time the team nails it, throw the spotlight on them. When the wheels fall off, step up, take the heat, and shield your team from unnecessary blame. It may feel quiet in the moment, but that kind of leadership echoes for a long time.

Tip 8: Choose Generosity: The Power of LGI versus MGI

He must not think answering my email is important. It's so clear that she doesn't care about my need. In moments of tension or conflict, we can all default to assuming the worst about others' intentions. I know in the rush-rush everyday of work life, I've certainly made that leap. But this is where the concepts of LGI (Least Generous Interpretation) and MGI (Most Generous Interpretation) come into play. LGI is when you interpret someone's actions in the most negative light possible, assuming bad intentions or negligence. MGI, on the other hand, is when you give them the benefit of the doubt, assuming positive intentions or understandable circumstances.

Just think, which one would you want to be measured against?!

Why LGI Hurts Teams

Let's say your coworker Rahul doesn't respond to your voicemail. With LGI, your mind might leap to "Rahul's ignoring me because he has no respect for our department or our issue." By 5 p.m., frustration has festered and your blood pressure's practically doing burpees. *But the reality?* Rahul spent the day in back-to-back meetings, preparing a detailed presentation to support your project in front of senior leadership.

In this case, assuming the worst only led to unnecessary stress and potential conflict. Rahul was actually working hard on your behalf, and LGI turned a nonissue into a source of inner churn and friction.

How MGI Builds Trust

Now, imagine approaching the same scenario with MGI: "Rahul's probably swamped and hasn't had a chance to reply." This interpretation fosters patience, empathy, and understanding. (Your nervous system might thank you for it, too). When Rahul finally connects with you and explains his day, your response is likely to be one of appreciation (or at minimum, acceptance) rather than resentment. When you go with MGI, you're setting the tone for a culture where people trust each other, speak up honestly, and don't have to worry about being judged for it. Other examples of MGI might sound like "I'm sure there's a valid explanation for this; I'll give them the benefit of the doubt," "I'll assume positive intent until I have more information," or even "Let's approach this with the understanding that unexpected things can happen."

Sometimes, we need a humbling moment to remind us that things aren't always as they seem. I remember a time when a marketing assistant on my team started delivering work that felt shoddier than usual. I was frustrated and ready to address it with her, but something stopped me. When I finally raised the issue, a little annoyed, she opened up. She was distracted, struggling with personal crises—she'd just begun the process of a difficult divorce and had learned her best friend had a terminal diagnosis. I had no idea. It was a moment of clarity for me, reminding me how easy it is to assume the worst without understanding the full picture. Call it a teachable moment in giving people space and understanding during tough times, and a reminder that a little understanding can go a long way.

The Ripple Effect of Generosity

MGI is a strategic choice that strengthens team cohesion and resilience. When leaders practice MGI, they're modeling everyday empathy, and others are more inclined to mimic the behavior. People give each other grace during stressful times. That helps ease tension before it turns into conflict, creating a more supportive, steady team vibe.

Practical Ways to Practice MGI

- **Pause before reacting.** When faced with a situation that could spark frustration or an all-out tantrum, pause for a moment. Ask yourself, "What's a neutral or positive explanation for this?"

- **Ask questions first.** Instead of jumping to conclusions, inquire. A simple "Hey, I'm sure you're busy. I noticed you haven't responded—everything okay?" can open the door to more understanding.

- **Reflect on intentions.** Remind yourself that most people don't intend to harm or neglect others. Everyone's doing the best they can with what they've got.

While MGI is a powerful tool, it's not a blanket pass for all behavior. If you see patterns of subpar work or poor communication, of course you need to address these constructively. MGI helps in avoiding unnecessary conflict but doesn't mean ignoring genuine issues.

Choose Generosity, Reap the Rewards

Want to lean more into MGI? At its core, it's turning "judging" into "understanding." It cuts stress, builds trust, and makes your team stronger and more productive. If you're tired of jumping to conclusions, try generosity—it'll change the energy.

Tip 9: A Spark in the Darkness: Appreciative Inquiry

When Elise, a coaching client and senior manager at a tech company, lost half her team in a brutal re-org, I don't have to tell you that morale sank. She described her remaining team as "adrift," looking vacant and lost and not even sure what they stood for anymore.

Elise, a natural doer, wanted to dive into fixing things immediately. But I encouraged her to try something different this time: Appreciative Inquiry (yup, the other AI!).[3]

This powerful, strengths-focused framework was developed by Dr. David Cooperrider and Dr. Suresh Srivastva at Case Western Reserve University. It could enable her team to find their footing— not by obsessing over what was broken or failed, but by identifying and grounding themselves in what was already working well.

Appreciative Inquiry prompts us to spot what's working, as in *What are we doing well? How can we build on that?* In fact, Dr. Barbara Fredrickson at the University of Michigan found in her research that helping people reach joy and contentment (states that are fueled by Appreciative Inquiry) *doubles* peoples' openness to possibilities, while being in states of fear and anger narrows our thoughts and actions. This strengths focus is called the "broaden-and-build" effect, boosting creativity, problem-solving, and resilience. Sounds nice, doesn't it?![4]

So Elise started with two simple but profound questions during her next one-on-ones: "What practices around here do we want to hold on to and preserve?" and "When you picture our team at its absolute best, what are we doing differently?" What followed was pretty epic.

Turning the Lens to Strengths

Elise's team began naming the habits that were working for them. One person highlighted that their weekly "Wins and Lessons" practice (which had been neglected during the re-org) was a meaningful space for reflecting and problem-solving. Another emphasized the flexibility and consideration the team practiced in managing their work-life flow, which they felt was essential to maintain.

The second question, "When you picture our team at its absolute best, what are we doing differently?" led to forward-looking ideas. Suggestions included continuing with structured quarterly reviews of team processes but improving them to identify inefficiencies and broadening existing decision-making protocols to include new scenarios the team faced. Most important, they named the need to keep their communication mechanisms but add strategic-level updates to provide greater visibility into changing company priorities and goals.

These ideas weren't pie-in-the-sky. They were doable. And deeply connected to the team's values. They became the foundation for the team's roadmap to move forward. When Elise brought these responses to the whole group and started acting on them, a new identity and mission started to emerge.

From Inquiry to Action

Here's a key ingredient of Appreciative Inquiry (and nope, it's not sriracha): Appreciative Inquiry shouldn't just stop at discovering what's working. *Turn those conversations into action.* For Elise, the first step was resurrecting the Friday "Wins and Lessons" ritual, which was easy to implement and resulted in instant smiles, a reminder of why people loved it in the first place. She also piloted a "team reset day" to hit pause on the daily grind, regroup, and brainstorm ways to tackle long-term goals. Her team vibe was starting to feel less like post-re-org weariness and chaos and more like "We've got this."

Ready to Try It?

Appreciative Inquiry comes in handy when your team is experiencing organizational change or morale challenges, or when you want to help rebuild the team's identity. Test it yourself and try asking those two questions at your next meeting:

1. What practices do we want to hold on to and preserve?
2. When you picture our team at its absolute best, what are we doing differently?

Then listen. Resist the urge to fix or judge. You might be surprised by the strengths and solutions hiding in plain sight. It's like lighting a candle in a dark room: Suddenly, you can see possibilities that were totally invisible before.

6 Self-Care

Mastering the Art of Self-Preservation

You've probably heard it all before. Yoga, meditation, a nice bath with aromatherapy—everyone seems to have their "fix" for burnout. But you know what? No amount of eucalyptus oil or Zen playlists will make the weight of burnout disappear. *Real* self-care is about understanding what really fuels you—and on the other side, what drives you into the ground. Then we need to tackle those things head-on. (Spoiler alert: Your fuel is more than just your 4 p.m. coffee habit; it's your mindset too.)

We're going deeper than once-a-year resolutions and quick fixes that only provide temporary relief. You'll explore how to navigate the pressure of your *own* expectations and the drive to always do more and be more. After all, the "must-get-it-right" mindset can be just as taxing as looming deadlines. And when you're also managing the needs of everyone around you—work, family, friends—it's easy to feel pulled in every direction and need a moment (or week!) to just be. *Turns out trying to be everything to everyone isn't a sustainable job description.* We're talking about setting into motion those self-care actions that make a genuine difference, then reinforcing them until they become second nature.

In this chapter, we'll explore what it really means to care for yourself beyond a place of obligation, but because it actually makes your life and work better. You'll reflect on when and how you thrive, and start putting into practice the kinds of habits that genuinely sustain you for the long haul. Now's the time to shift your mindset, recognize patterns that keep you stuck, and reclaim your focus, energy, and purpose. No matter how overwhelming it may feel at times, the good news is that you have the power to make meaningful change. So let's get real about what's going on beneath the surface (and who knows, maybe we can even do it with a chuckle, turning some of life's chaos into a punchline or two).

Tip 1: Protect Your Peace

Leadership brings noise. Not just in the literal sense of meetings, pinging notifications, and the constant hum of door knocks, but also in its mental weight. People look to you for decisions, guidance, and sometimes even emotional support, and the noise can become blaring fast. If you're not careful, it can drown out your ability to focus and innovate, and, let's be honest, you can come *this close* to throwing your laptop out the window!

Protecting your peace means preserving the mental and emotional energy you need to lead effectively. Just think: The calmer you are, the better you'll think, the clearer you'll communicate, and the more grounded your team will feel. Because here's the secret: *Your energy sets the tone for everyone else.*

Decline the Drains

We've talked about being the sh!t umbrella for your team, but who's shielding you? While saying "yes" to requests for your time might feel like the right or responsible thing to do, it's guaranteed to leave you with zero time to actually think, strategize, or, you know, lead!

Here's a bold move: Be openly judicious with your time rather than quiet or apologetic about it. What do I mean? *Decline the meeting. Ask for the meeting agenda before saying yes. Tell people you'll need to look at your commitments and get back to them. Say "no" more.* One eye-opening study supports this, finding that when employees were able to be more selective about meeting attendance—specifically when meetings were reduced by 40%—employee productivity was 71% higher. This is because study subjects felt more empowered and more ownership over their to-do lists, which increased their satisfaction by 52%.[1] Fewer meetings and more flow? Yes!

You can also set expectations *with your team* about using time well. encourage them to come to you with solutions to problems to workshop together, and when you do need to gather as a team, keep an eye toward brevity. A 15-minute stand-up meeting can often accomplish more than an hour-long roundtable of overexplaining.

Turn Off the Ping Parade

Slack. Teams. Email. Texts. DMs. Reminders. You could probably drop a club remix with all the pings and buzzes that hit you in a single hour! Leaders need to be responsive and available eventually, but it *doesn't* follow that you have to respond to every notification right away. If you're constantly reactive, you'll never have the space to be proactive. That's why focus hours are nonnegotiable.

Block off time on your calendar when you're unavailable for interruptions and mark your status as Do Not Disturb for those times. (Remember, the only magic fairy with the power to turn on Do Not Disturb is you.) You're modeling healthy boundaries for your team, not ignoring them. Share your focus hours with others so they understand when it's best to approach you and when they need to solve things independently. Pro tip: If you're worried about missing something urgent, set up a single point of contact (like an assistant or a designated team member) for critical issues during your "off-the-grid" times.

Build Micro-Moments of Recharge

Now, you don't need a week-long yoga retreat in Bali to recharge (though if you can swing it, I surely won't stop you). Sometimes, it's implementing everyday moments where you have some slack to recalibrate.

For example, take short, regular breaks throughout your day: time to take a walk, grab a coffee, walk out on a patio, and stand in silence. And while responding to texts from good friends and loved ones can count, mindless scrolling social media doesn't. Truly recharging means restoring your nervous system, rather than just "not working for a few minutes."

My simple go-tos for recharging are going for an outdoor run in my neighborhood (when I can) before the bulk of my day begins, taking work breaks like texting a friend or sibling to check in or send them something funny, looking for a recipe online for an upcoming meal, or having a good look out my window while I stand and do some stretches. How about you?

Once you think of your own short list, treat these moments as sacred appointments with yourself. They're not frivolous.

Your Calm Is Contagious

Guarding your time and energy isn't just for you—it creates a healthier, more focused team. So set the vibe. Turn down the volume on the noise and turn up your focus. You've got people to lead and peace to protect.

Tip 2: Deposits and Withdrawals: Managing Your Energy Bank Account

You know when your phone dies because you ignored the low battery warning? It's a sinking, exasperating feeling, realizing you've run out of power at a not-great moment. And the worst part? You knew better than to let it happen!

Leadership is no different. For sure it's demanding, but trying to lead from a place of exhaustion isn't sustainable or effective. To handle the hard stuff with heart—like I'm challenging you to do throughout this book—you've got to prioritize restoring, renewing, and refreshing yourself. So let's talk about how to keep your energy and battery charged up.

Put Yourself Back on the Calendar

Picture your calendar. It's likely filled with back-to-back meetings, tasks, and requests from others. But where are *you* in all of that? If you're not blocking time for yourself, you're effectively saying your well-being doesn't matter as much as everything else. That's not just unsustainable—it's a recipe for resentment.

"You time" isn't selfish; it's strategic. Whether it's brainstorming, tinkering, reading, putting together a Lego, or pacing while you have a good think, find the activities that help you clear your mind or use it as its sharpest. Then schedule them like you would an important meeting (and vow not to "just check your email real quick" during these meetings!). Because guess what? They *are* important commitments, with the person responsible for keeping everything running: you.

Recharging Isn't Optional

Leaders often convince themselves that self-care is a luxury they can't afford. Deadlines loom, teams need support, and there's always one more email to answer. But—and this is a big but—if you don't recharge, your body and mind will force you to, through burnout, illness, or disengagement.

Think of recharging regularly at work as care and maintenance. We humans don't have unending, magically regenerating energy supplies.

By injecting rest and renewal into your day, you ensure you have the capacity to lead today and tomorrow with a clear head and purpose.

Audit Your Energy Spenders

Think of your energy like a bank account at work. Withdraw too much without making deposits, and you'll end up overdrawn—aka burned out and irritable. You can start by doing an inventory, beginning with meetings: How many of them could have been emails (*three-sentence ones!*)? How many are you attending out of habit rather than necessity? It's taken me a while, but I've come to see declining unnecessary meetings as responsible, not rude.

Next, tackle notifications. Slack pings, email alerts, and app notifications are like mosquitos—small, constant distractions that sap your focus. Turn 'em off during focus hours and watch how much energy you save.

Third, audit your calendar. For example, color-code what can be delegated to someone else in blue. Add your recurring uninterrupted time blocks in green. Put communal time like office hours in orange. See how you're prioritizing and pacing your energy now? You can't be strategic about your "time spend" if you're unaware of what's on the calendar.

Lead by Example

Protecting your energy is good for your team and you. When they see you have limits, it gives them permission to do the same.

True leadership is showing up as your best self and inspiring others to follow. When you take control of your energy, you're not merely surviving the grind, you're building momentum for long-term success.

So what's your first deposit?

Tip 3: Pace Yourself: Leadership Is a Marathon, Not a Sprint

Leadership is like running a long race. And as a distance runner myself (an extremely slow one, but hey, I show up!), we always tell first-timers: *Respect the distance*. If you try to go too hard, too fast, you'll burn out before the halfway point.

Leading is just like that. At the start of a new initiative, adrenaline tempts you to rush ahead, but seasoned leaders know better. They conserve energy, find a steady rhythm, and avoid the trap of letting excitement or high-pressure moments drain their reserves.

Pacing yourself doesn't need to be rigid, though. What's most important is that you're aware of your needs and adjusting as you go. To help you with that, here are some of my favorite questions to help you set a sustainable pace:

- Am I saving energy for what matters?
- Do I lean on my team to share the load?
- Where will my energy deliver the biggest ROI in three days, three weeks, or three months?
- Am I overcommitting to the wrong priorities?

These questions are simple but powerful. They'll help you stay in tune with yourself and focus on what really matters in the long run. I recommend scheduling a monthly check-in with yourself, an accountability partner, or a coach to run through them.

Delegate Like a Pro (aka Build Your Support Crew)

No one runs a marathon without support—that's why there's hydration stations, pacers, and the cheering crowd. So why would you lead without leaning on your team? Enter delegation. A chance to let your team shine while you're freed up to work on what counts.

But delegation only works if you let go of the need for perfection. Trust your team to do the job in their way, even if it doesn't look exactly like how you'd do it. The overarching goal here isn't to control; it's to use all the resources available to you, smartly.

Set Deadlines, Not Burnout Traps

People get sick, technology fails, and surprises happen. So set realistic deadlines with room for surprises.

If you chronically underestimate how long things take (as I've been known to do), share with your team that you're working on that and invite them to challenge you if a deadline seems unrealistic. You can test out phrases like these:

- "I'm working on improving my time estimates. If this deadline feels tight, let me know."
- "I tend to underestimate timelines, so feel free to speak up if you think we're pushing it."
- "I'm committed to being more realistic with my estimates, so please let me know if you think we're off track."
- "I know I can be overly optimistic about timelines, so your feedback is crucial here."

Refuel Along the Way: Mantras to Lead By

Leadership can be a long haul, so give yourself the same care you'd offer your team. These quick, grounding phrases can help you stay centered and steady, especially when the pace picks up:

- **"Save some for the climb."**

  You don't have to use up all your energy in the first stretch.
- **"Sustain, don't strain."**

  Keep a pace you can maintain, not one that leaves you burned out.

- **"Steady wins the day."**

    Focus beats frantic. Consistency is its own power move!

- **"Progress over perfection."**

    Small steps still count. Keep moving.

- **"Rest is part of the strategy."**

    Breaks aren't indulgent; they're necessary.

- **"Refuel now, not after the crash."**

    Waiting until you're fully depleted helps no one.

- **"Even the Concorde still had to land and refuel."**

    Enough said.

Pick one or two that resonate and return to them when you need to reset your focus or give yourself permission to pause.

Steady Progress, Collective Triumph

Respecting the distance, delegating wisely, and telling yourself the right stories—those actions build a team that thrives and paves the way to success. But the real victory? Crossing the finish line together, ready for what's next.

Tip 4: Practice Mindfulness Moments

Oof … I don't like remembering the day I met "Tim" twice. I was attending the Thinkers50 event in London, a gathering of some of the brightest minds in business. Picture fancy chandeliers, impeccably dressed professionals, and excitement in the air. The thing is, I wasn't 100% present.

Between jet lag, a sick kid at home, and the overwhelming stimulation of being surrounded by so many business rockstars, my brain was in overdrive.

And then, the cringe moment. I shook hands with a friendly guy who introduced himself as Tim. When I replied, "Oh, you look so familiar," he chuckled. "Yep … we met earlier today at the breakfast event." My face flushed while my internal monologue screeched, "Time to move to a new planet!"

That interaction haunted me all day. I realized I couldn't connect, experience, or enjoy much if I wasn't present. That moment was big for me because I realized: I can't control the circumstances, but I can do my best *to be where I am* despite everything else that's going on.

Start Small, See Big Results

Leadership often feels fast-paced, stimulating, and nonstop, like my event. But mindfulness is your "back to the present" button. Is it a retreat to a mountaintop or finding an hour of silence? Actually, it can look a lot smaller. One study published in the *British Journal of Health Psychology*, found that just 10 minutes of daily mindfulness practice can improve well-being, ease depression and anxiety, and help people to be more motivated.[2]

So how can you create small, intentional resets? Here are a few helpful practices:

- **Box breathing:** Before an event, meeting, or tough conversation, take five deep breaths. Inhale for four seconds, hold for four, exhale for four, and hold again for four. It clears the mental fog.

- **Walk it out:** Take a quick, intentional walk. Leave your phone behind or turned off in your pocket. Make a point to focus on the sound of your footsteps, the feel of the breeze, or the colors around you.

- **The awkward pose:** Strike an intentionally awkward pose, like pretending you're Superman or standing on one leg flamingo-style.

Hold it for 10 seconds. This odd physical reset gets you out of your head. It's hard to spiral about work stress when you're standing like a pink bird!

- **Tension rewrite:** Give your tension a personality. For example, if you're frowning and your jaw is tight, imagine it's a grumpy character who refuses to relax. Name it (like "Grumpy Greg"), then talk to it ("Hey, Greg, let's work on letting it go"), and then consciously release it. Silly? Yes. But reframing stress helps you get past it. Plus, if Greg can chill, so can you!

- **The invisible hand:** When you're feeling overwhelmed, place your hands palm-down on your desk, pushing all the "weight" of your frustration—hard—into the desk. Imagine it's absorbing all your stress like a magnet. Then, flip your hands palm-up, snapping your palms up as if you're letting the stress go. It's a quick, subtle ritual that releases stress.

- **Three-word mental anchor:** Pick three words that help you come back to now, such as *Be Here Now, Embrace the Present,* or *Here. Now. Breathe.* Repeat them silently like a reassuring directive as you inhale and exhale.

Make It a Team Sport

Mindfulness helps more than you; it impacts everyone around you. Weave it into your leadership approach in small ways—for example, by asking an overwhelmed team member, "What would help you reset right now?" Or pause a meeting to ask, "How is everyone feeling right now?" You could also practice starting meetings with everyone taking a few deep breaths or sighing audibly to get fully present. Sometimes a simple question invites a moment of reflection, and that shift can reenergize the room.

And if you're too busy right now to get the gist of what I'm saying and want the three-word summary, here you go: *Press Reset Often!*

Tip 5: Build Your Village

Leadership can be a lonely gig. You're constantly making decisions, solving problems, and managing expectations—lots of times without much external validation or support. So how do you keep going when the weight of leadership feels heavy?

The remedy lies in building your village.

Think of your village as a carefully curated group of people who have your back: peers, mentors, or fellow leaders who get the challenges you face. They've probably been where you are and can offer input and encouragement—and heck, maybe even a good laugh to help you get perspective.

Peer Power

One of the best places to start building your village is with your peers. These are people who don't just nod politely when you vent; they've been through similar trials, which allows you to connect and bond. Supporting this, one study found that 94% of employees are more productive when they felt connected to their colleagues. Not just that, but employees who feel connected to peers are half as likely to leave within the next year and four times as likely to say they are very satisfied at their jobs.[3]

To identify good peer relationships, start with some of these questions:

- *Who in your circle has faced similar leadership struggles?*
- *Who do you trust to challenge your assumptions or help you think through tough decisions?*
- *Who has the experience and empathy to help you get unstuck?*

From there, starting conversations with this group might sound like:

- "I've been facing this challenge with my team lately. How have you approached something similar?"
- "When you're managing [XYZ project], what helps you stay grounded?"
- "I'd love to get your perspective on [ABC]. I'm feeling a bit stuck."

By being the one to initiate these kinds of conversations, you'll grow your social confidence (*hello, bonus benefit!*) and you'll also soon find the peers who will be the most supportive, realistic, and honest with you. These are the ones who give you a friendly nudge while also having your back when the going gets tough.

Mentors: Learn from Experience

A good mentor helps you avoid their own mistakes, challenges your thinking, and provides perspective on the bigger picture. But mentorship doesn't have to be formal. Try starting with finding someone who's invested in your growth.

To start, ask yourself:

- *Who do I admire for their leadership or approach?*
- *Who's walked a path relevant to mine and can offer insights?*
- *Is there someone who pushes me to think beyond my current limits?*

Once you've identified them, you can ask them questions like:

- "I'm struggling with XYZ. I'd love to hear how you handled something similar."

- "What advice would you give to a leader trying to navigate ABC?"
- "What's the one thing about XYZ you wish you'd known earlier in your leadership journey?"

See the simplicity of it? You've got the go-to questions and phrases. Now it's up to you to take that first courageous step to start the conversation.

Rising Stars: Grow Together

Sometimes the most surprising support comes from rising stars, the future leaders in your network. They may lack experience, but their fresh perspective and drive can remind you why you started leading, and asking for their input will be a boost to them, too. You could ask them:

- "How would you approach [specific challenge] differently than I might?"
- "What's one thing you wish more leaders understood about X?"
- "What's a fresh perspective or idea you've been thinking about that could boost our products/process/culture?"

Make time to listen to their ideas, collaborate on projects, and challenge each other to think bigger. I once saw a manager consult a rising star about resistance he was getting from younger employees toward HR benefit changes. That rising star shared openly with the manager about the pushback and why it was happening. Mind you, it required HR to tweak their approach too—but by addressing younger workers' concerns and better involving them in the process, that manager turned the resistance into engagement. Cultivate these relationships, internally and externally, and watch both of you rise together.

The Strength of Vulnerability: Share Your Struggles

One of the biggest benefits of building your village is the opportunity to share your struggles without fear of judgment. So let me really underline it for you: You're allowed to lean on others for support!

And remember, building your village is a long game. It's one thing to have a huge network of people who barely know your name, but it's far more meaningful to invest in and nurture deep, meaningful relationships with those who truly understand the demands of leadership. Now's the time to lean in, open up, and let your village do what it does best: support you.

Tip 6: For the Love of All Things, Take Your PTO

Color me shocked that the most viral video I ever posted is one where I urge people to take their paid time off. Let me say, *I'm passionate about this*! It absolutely struck a nerve. And guess what? It's still relevant. Leaders, we have to stop treating PTO like it's some sort of emergency fallback. It's not a reward for grinding hard; it's a way to sustain yourself. It's a long-term strategy to make sure you don't burn out, and a chance to be the kind of leader who models actual wellness, not martyrdom.

Stop Treating PTO Like a Painkiller—It's a Vitamin

Listen up. If you're waiting until your body forces you to take PTO because you're at a breaking point, you're doing it wrong. PTO isn't a painkiller we earn from toiling—it's a vitamin. It's there to keep you healthy *before* you hit burnout. If you only take it when you're completely wiped, it's too late. See it as preventive care, not playing catch-up with your own sanity.

A lot of leaders treat PTO like a "last resort" when they've hit their tipping point—or they humblebrag about how much PTO they're banking and rolling into the next year. But if you're frayed, you're not leading at your best, and your team sees it. And they feel it.

Unplug for Real

I know a lot of you still check your emails and answer calls when you're supposed to be off. I know because I've done it too. One study by the US Travel Association found that the higher up you are, the greater the expectation to work on vacation. Executive and senior leaders (44%) feel the highest expectation to work during time off compared to managers (34%) and nonmanagers (21%).[4] FYI, this is unhealthy.

The whole point of taking time off is to actually unplug. That means no emails. No Slack. No getting dragged into random Zoom meetings from the hotel lobby. Plan for your time out, then trust that the team can handle things without you.

Start getting in the habit of saying things like "I'm off the clock," "I'll be out of touch from X to Y," or "I'll respond when I'm back." I've found these can become deeply liberating. Use these phrases to reinforce the boundary between work and rest. You might feel tempted to check in, but saying these out loud can help shift your mindset.

See unplugging as a needed skill. And if you don't practice it, your brain never gets the rest it needs to innovate, problem-solve, and lead effectively. So take your PTO and get used to saying, "I'll be back on email on X date." Then follow through.

Don't Ask Your Team for Reasons

Here's a pro tip: When your team takes PTO, don't ask them, "What are you going to do with your time off?" "Have something fun planned?" or "What's the reason code?" It's none of your business. Their time off is theirs to enjoy however they see fit—that's why they call 'em personal days, after all. Whether they're having a highly personal medical procedure, lying on the couch eating chips, or going on a much-needed adventure, it doesn't matter. They don't owe you an explanation.

The only thing you need to say is "Got it," "Thanks for letting me know," or "Noted," with a smile. That's it. Period. End of story. Everyone deserves the space to take care of themselves without fear of judgment.

Recharge by Example

If you want your team to embrace PTO, lead by example. Don't be the boss who never takes time off; there's no trophy for your "record" in the end. Realize that burnout is contagious, but so is wellness. Take breaks, talk about the benefits, and show that time off fuels better performance. As leadership expert John Maxwell says, "A leader is one who knows the way, goes the way, and shows the way."

Tip 7: Celebrate Small Wins

A wise man once said, "Success isn't a destination; it's the daily grind." That man was Dwayne "The Rock" Johnson and he's got a point. We tend to think success is a grand event—the big promotion, the game-changing deal, the industry award with the overpriced banquet dinner. But waiting for those once-in-a-blue-moon victories? That's a guaranteed way to miss out, *and fizzle out*, before you ever get to the finish line.

In my coaching practice, I find that those most prone to this wait-to-celebrate style are achievers who are hard on themselves or set over-the-top standards. And yet our sense of determination and esteem is often built in the small moments—the incremental wins, the "We survived the client presentation" fist bumps and the "We somehow pulled off that demon project" deep sighs of relief. Small wins keep people engaged, energized, and most importantly, willing to keep pushing forward.

So, as a leader, here's your job: Recognize the mini-milestones. Celebrate the progress, whether that's with a round of applause or high-fives, surprise cupcakes, or a heartfelt thank you. Make work feel rewarding in real time, not just in some far-off, future "we made it" moment.

One thing I do to celebrate small wins is to follow up with my assistant about to-dos she took care of that had a positive ripple. She may not know the full impact of something quick or seemingly transactional that she helped me with, but celebrating at the start of our meetings with something she did and how it strengthened a relationship, moved our mission forward, or helped us win a new client changes the tone of everything. It's extremely satisfying to hear her say, "Oh wow, that's so cool that led to something bigger!"

The Psychology of Small Wins (or Why Our Brains Love a Little Party)

There's actual science behind this, so by all means use it an excuse to eat cake on a Tuesday. Studies show that when we acknowledge small wins, our brains release dopamine, the feel-good chemical that keeps us motivated. It's the same hit of satisfaction you get when you check something off your to-do list (which is also why some of us write things down *after* we've done them just for the thrill of crossing them out—no shame, people).

For teams, this translates into momentum. When people see progress, they stay engaged. When they feel recognized, they stay committed. And when they associate work with positive reinforcement instead of just pressure and deadlines? They actually want to keep contributing at their best.

"But I Don't Want to Hand Out Gold Stars Just for Breathing"

Fair. Over-celebrating can turn into a participation trophy free-for-all where praise starts to feel meaningless. That's not what we're going for here.

The key is *thoughtful recognition*. A well-placed "Nice analysis, Rita—talk about a well-thought-out approach!" or a "That was an insightful point you made in the meeting, Ahmed" goes a long way. And if your team just pulled off something significant—even if it's not major-project-launch level, acknowledge it.

Here are a few ways to celebrate without making it weird:

- **The casual shoutout:** A Slack message, a quick email, or a moment in a meeting to say, "Hey, this is report is awesome. I was especially impressed with …" Simple. Free. Effective.

- **The "skip-a-meeting" pass:** Hand out a golden ticket (real or digital) that lets someone opt out of a noncritical meeting of their choice. Label it "Because you have better things to do."

- **The permission slip:** Give them a block of time back for personal use. Let them leave early on a Friday or take a guilt-free, post-work-travel break to recharge.

- **The fun ritual:** Create a team tradition for wins, like ringing a bell, passing around a ridiculous trophy, or adding a micro-victory to a "Wall of Wins."

One client of mine had so much fun with the wall of wins concept, they started a "What Happens Next?" game. They sparked some fun and lightheartedness by leaving a whiteboard with a half-written story and let everyone add their own twist throughout the day. This wasn't about wins, obviously, but it did boost the team's spirits after they endured a tough year of turmoil.

The idea? Make progress visible. Recognize the wins, big or small, and you'll keep momentum strong and motivation high, even in tough times.

Tip 8: Call a Spade a Spade, and a Workaholic a Workaholic

Somewhere along the way, we started glorifying workaholism like it's an Olympic sport. Some employees flex about pulling all-nighters like they're battle scars. Leaders set a certain tone by sending emails at midnight. And—confession time—many of us feel a weird sense of pride in being *indispensable* (translation: overworked and stretched thinner than a dollar-store paper towel).

But long-term workaholism isn't a strategy; it's a slow-motion train wreck. It means that burnout, resentment, and, oddly, lower productivity are near. If you want your team to thrive, you need to kill the myth that always being "on" is the only way to succeed.

Redefining Productivity: It's Not Just About Hours

If working more hours actually equaled better results, we'd all be thriving. But study after study shows that beyond a certain point, longer hours lead to diminishing returns. Physical and mental exhaustion, decision fatigue, and stress all pile up, making you less creative, less engaged, and more error-prone.

What if instead of measuring productivity by hours clocked in, we measured it by energy, focus, and meaningful contributions? What if we celebrated impact over exhaustion? Imagine how different workplaces would feel if leaders set the expectation that time *off* is just as valuable as time *on*.

Set Boundaries ... and Actually Respect Them

It's one thing to extol "setting boundaries," but it's an entirely different thing to actually model and live it. You might tell your team to log off at 6 while you're still sending Slack messages at 11 at night. But guess what? That sends a mixed message. You need to teach and lead by example.

Try this instead:

- **Declare work-free zones.** No emails or calls outside of designated hours. If it's not an emergency, it's waiting.

- **Encourage (real) lunch breaks.** This requires actually stepping away from your desk, not inhaling a sandwich over unread emails.

- **Stop rewarding overwork.** If the same people are always "staying late to show dedication," it's time to reassess workloads, not praise them for their sacrifice.

- **Take your own advice.** If you tell your team to rest but you're always burning the midnight oil, guess what? They won't believe you. Model what balance looks like.

Boundaries like these have the benefit of making your team a place where people of all lifestyles can thrive. Many people have caregiving responsibilities that mean they really can't overwork, even if they wanted to. Taking "overworking" off the table as a desirable trait ensures that everyone is expected to contribute appropriately, and no more or less than that.

At Dinner, Bring Your Appetite, Not Your Inbox

This skill set also requires you to set boundaries for your *brain*. Workaholism isn't just physical exhaustion; it's mental overdrive. You might not be at your desk, but if you're prone to replaying that meeting argument while trying to enjoy dinner with your family, you're still working.

Here's how to mentally clock out:

- **Have a transition ritual.** Whether it's a quick walk, changing clothes, a shower, or shutting your laptop with dramatic flair, find a physical way to signal to your brain that work is *done*.

- **Don't let work live rent-free in your head.** If a thought pops up after hours, jot it down and promise yourself you'll handle it tomorrow. Then let it go. I like to keep a page in my phone's Notes app just for this purpose.

- **Create a "no work zone" at home.** Designate a physical space in your home where work doesn't belong: the couch, living room, the kitchen table, or even just a corner of the room. This helps your mind create a boundary between work and relaxation, which is especially important for those who work from home. (Yup, I'm talking to all the Domestic-Dining-Table Dynamos out there. Give yourself permission to be free).

- **Use a "done for the day" statement.** Verbally declare in your head (or even out loud if that's your thing) that you're done for the day. Saying something like "Work is finished, and now it's time for me" sets a clear mental and emotional boundary between work and personal time.

- **Set a mental curfew.** No checking emails or Slack after a certain hour. Protect your evenings like you would an important meeting.

Living Well Is the Real Power Move

People-first leaders know that a rested, engaged, and energized team will always outperform a burned-out, overworked one. So stop treating workaholism like a compliment. Call it what it is, and then do the brave thing: Make work *just one part* of a full, meaningful life.

Tip 9: No Is a Form of Self-Respect

Let's talk about boundaries. Not the weather-worn, wooden kind like you'd find in my backyard that need fixing, but the kind that keep you focused and spending your time well. If you want to survive—no, *thrive*—as a leader, you have to get real about your limits. Let's establish once and for all, you do not need to (1) be endlessly available, (2) say yes to everything, or (3) burn yourself to a crisp trying to please everyone. A big part of the solution is about knowing where you end and where your team begins.

Why Leaders Need Boundaries (Yes, Even You)

You know that feeling when your calendar is so packed that even a bathroom break requires strategic planning? (Cue my yuck face.) That's the universe (and your nervous system) begging you to set some boundaries. Leaders who don't set boundaries end up with their time and energy up for grabs, where they're constantly in reactive mode—functioning like a crisis hotline, responding to every Slack ping like it's a life-or-death situation, and losing the ability to think clearly and strategically.

Boundaries allow you to focus on what actually matters. They give you the space to lead rather than just manage chaos. They also help your team more confidently guard their time. And trust me, a team that knows when to log off, protect their energy, and set limits is a team that performs better in the long run.

How to Communicate Boundaries Without Sounding Like a Jerk

A lot of leaders avoid setting boundaries because they're afraid of looking uncommitted or selfish. But boundaries aren't stone walls to keep people out. They're more like guardrails to keep you protected. And when communicated well, they actually make you *more* effective and respected.

Ways to Set Boundaries Clearly and Professionally

- **Acknowledge the request.** "I appreciate the invitation, but I won't be able to make it this time." (Takeaway: I don't need to overexplain to decline.)

- **Protect your time.** "I'm happy to discuss this, but let's set up a time when I can give it my full attention." (Takeaway: No, I will not drop everything right this second for a popup request.)

- **Honor your deep work.** "I protect my deep work time in the mornings, so let's touch base in the afternoon." (Takeaway: My brain needs space to function, so please respect my needs and rhythms.)

- **Set digital boundaries.** "I won't be checking email over the weekend, but I'll get back to you first thing Monday." (Takeaway: My rest is nonnegotiable.)

- **Define meeting-free hours.** "I have standing no-meeting hours from 9 to 11 a.m. to focus on strategic work. If it's urgent, let's connect afterward." (Takeaway: Uninterrupted time equals better decisions.)

- **Control your availability.** "I'll be offline for the next few hours. Can we catch up another time?" (Takeaway: Just because I'm here doesn't mean I'm available.)

Voilà! These are key sentence-starters in the boundary-setters vocabulary. Use 'em and refine 'em.

Boundaries: The Key to Sustainable Leadership

Leaders who protect their time, energy, and mental clarity make better decisions, support their teams more effectively, and actually enjoy their work instead of dreading it.

Start now. Choose one small but meaningful boundary to reinforce this week and watch how it transforms your leadership.

7 Psychological Safety

Making Team Fearlessness a Thing

Fear shrinks ideas. It stifles voices. It makes people second-guess their brilliance before it ever sees daylight. And in too many workplaces, fear still has the mic.

It doesn't have to stay that way. Psychological safety isn't some mystery. It's something leaders can actively create. When people feel safe to speak up, take risks, and be human, they stop holding back. That's when trust deepens, creativity flows, and the team begins to unlock its full potential.

As a recovering perfectionist, I'm excited to tell you you don't have to be *perfect* to lead this way. You just have to be willing. In this chapter, we'll explore how you can make your team feel safe enough to experiment, push boundaries, brainstorm, dig deeper, and speak up even if they're less than polished while doing it.

One of the most thrilling turning points in my work advising teams is seeing them experience a culture where fear is no longer the first reaction. You know you're starting to get it right when you see courage showing up in small, everyday behaviors. When you hear your team say things like "I'm going to take a risk here," or "I'm not sure about this, but I'll give it a shot," or even "Hey, I screwed this up, but here's what I learned." When you make it okay to fail and speak up, you're building confidence in taking risks and growing from them. Your team starts feeling safe to test ideas, refine their thinking, and move forward without fearing the fallout. And with every moment like this, they become bolder, more innovative, and more willing to stretch beyond what they thought was possible (even if it's just volunteering to lead a meeting without breaking into a cold sweat—progress!).

Let's figure out how to give people room to take a breath, take a chance, and try again. That kind of safety? It's how bold ideas move from maybe to *made it*.

Tip 1: Recognize Psychological Safety

Psychological safety is the quiet knowing that your ideas are valued, even if they're cockeyed, bold, or unconventional. Sounds nice to have that kind of freedom, right? But many leaders struggle to spot it when it's present.

So how do you recognize psychological safety when it's happening?

In teams with psychological safety (which we'll jump into in a sec), people feel comfortable taking interpersonal risks and speaking up, even when the conversation feels challenging. They can question assumptions, raise concerns, and admit mistakes without fear of backlash. These small but powerful behaviors create an environment where growth, risk-taking, and honest conversations can thrive.

And here's the quiet magic: When people feel safe, they start to show up with more heart. You'll hear more laughter. You'll see teammates leaning in to help each other without being asked. The whole room feels a little lighter, a little braver. Not just that, but did you know that employees who report a high level of psychological safety at work are more likely to engage in helping behaviors—and more likely to seek feedback from their peers?[1]

Here are the green flags to look for:

- **People speak up without fear.**

    This looks like: Team members challenge the status quo, raise concerns, and offer alternative approaches without hesitation. They trust that their input will be met with curiosity, not criticism.

    This sounds like: "I know this might be a stretch, but what if we tried X?" or "Here's an approach we haven't considered yet, and it might work because of Y." These are more than brainstorming phrases; they signal there's trust to say, *Humor me for a second while I go out on a limb....*

- **Mistakes are acknowledged openly.**

    This looks like: When mistakes happen, they're talked about without blame. Instead of defensiveness (or fear of being etched into the team's hall of shame!), there's a shared focus on learning and improving.

    This sounds like: "I made a technical mistake, but I'm pinpointing now where in the process it happened," or "That didn't work, but now we know what to change." Owning mistakes out loud and then being met with curiosity or understanding reminds the team that growth beats perfection.

- **People challenge each other constructively.**

    This looks like: Team members engage in disagreements that sharpen ideas rather than shut them down. There's a clear focus on improving outcomes, not defending egos.

    This sounds like: "I see your point, but have we considered this angle?" or "If we take that approach, I have a concern about ..." These moments create positive friction from critical thinking, helping you refine ideas together.

- **Leaders ask more questions than they answer.**

  This looks like: Instead of hogging airtime, leaders spread out opportunity, inviting others' ideas, making room for different perspectives, and resisting the urge to deliver a TED Talk at every meeting.

  This sounds like: "What's your perspective on this?" or "What concerns haven't we talked about yet?" A leader's curiosity sets the tone for everyone else to ask, explore, and push ideas forward.

- **Disagreements feel productive, not personal.**

  This looks like: Differences in opinion are allowed and voiced to find the best solution to the problem. People push back on ideas without making it about the person who shared them.

  This sounds like: "I see it differently, and here's why," or "Let's stress-test that assumption before we commit." The focus stays on strengthening solutions, not defending positions or giving someone the side eye.

Questioning Isn't Just Tolerated, It's Celebrated

In the most psychologically safe teams, questioning isn't an annoying disruption. It's looked at as a strength. So encourage your team members to be inquisitive. Meet their question with openness instead of eye rolls, and you'll notice more people actually *want* to speak up. That's when the best ideas surface. Turns out, curiosity really doesn't kill anything, it builds. (Now let's go deeper on it in the next tip!)

Tip 2: Curiosity Rules

Ever walked into a meeting where the air felt ... thick? Where asking a question seemed like it would set off a chain reaction? It's like everyone's waiting for someone else to say the thing, but no one wants to be the first. *If I question this, Carmen will think I'm not on her side,* or *It's probably safer to hang back so I don't step on Jim's toes,* or *Deirdre outranks me, so I'm keeping my mouth shut.* The worst part? It's not even about the topic anymore. It's about the unspoken rules that keep everyone quiet.

That silence? It's the sound of assumptions creeping in, unchecked. And assumptions are about as reliable as my uncle's old 1980s Chevy Caprice. (RIP to that lovable disaster of a car. Sure, it got us places, but it always broke down when we needed it most.) When your team's avoiding tough questions out of fear, yes—you're missing out on fresh perspectives but you're actively shutting down progress, burying risks, and turning problem-solving into a guessing game.

A team fueled by curiosity, on the other hand, asks questions like it's their job (because, frankly, it kind of is). They dig deeper. They challenge each other. They test assumptions before they cement them into strategy. And when that happens? That's when real progress kicks in.

Are We Asking Enough?

Before we get into why curiosity is the secret sauce of high-performing teams, ask yourself:

- When was the last time someone on your team asked, "What's a completely different way to approach this?"
- Do people admit when they don't know something, or do they nod like they understand and Google it later?
- Are brainstorming sessions actual idea-generating sprints, or just a performance of agreement?

If your answers make you cringe, you're not alone. Most teams don't ask enough. And it's costing them big. Curiosity isn't just a nice-to-have; it's a business advantage.

Teams That Ask, Win

When you lead with curiosity, you're signaling that *learning is constant, innovation is encouraged here,* and *we need fresh angles to tackle problems.* You're creating a culture where people can share, collaborate, and challenge the status quo, and where information moves openly (*not treated like some top-secret recipe only a few can access*). Encouraging curiosity means:

- **Better problem-solving:** Teams that ask, "What if?" find solutions faster than teams that assume they already know everything.

- **More innovation:** New ideas don't come from certainty; they come from exploring possibilities.

- **Stronger collaboration:** When people ask and listen rather than just wait for their turn to talk, they work together better.

The Questions That Change Everything

Want to shift your team culture? Start with these open-ended gems:

- *Instead of:* "Will this work?" *Try:* "What would make this work even better?"

- *Instead of:* "Who's responsible for this mistake?" *Try:* "What can we learn from this, and how do we prevent it next time?"

- *Instead of:* "Any questions?" (Cue silence.) *Try:* "What part of this could be clearer?"

Rather Than Simply Tolerating Questions, Celebrate Them

When your team starts asking questions, it's a sign they're engaged, thinking critically, and invested in what's next. Celebrate that! I still remember a manager who'd give a mischievous smile to my team and say, "Now we're talking!" whenever someone asked a bold question. It was like a green light for new thinking. Highlight when a tough, uncomfortable question has sparked a breakthrough. Make curiosity a part of your team's ordinary daily flow.

Curiosity kicks the door open and lets in fresh air. It turns a stale environment into a space where new ways of thinking can circulate. And it often brings back the vibrance. Welcome it.

Tip 3: Encourage Healthy Debate

On my early teams, debates weren't just common—they were practically a team sport. We were a bunch of management consultants who treated meetings like a chance to spar and out-logic each other. *We could've taught lawyers a thing or two about loving a good argument!* For all the whiteboard battles, though, not every conversation was productive.

But healthy debate? That's a whole different skill. It's the kind of productive tension where ideas bounce, evolve, and become stronger together. It's the spark that turns a good plan into a great one. It's *never* about shutting someone down; it's about making the conversation or solution better.

The best teams expect and invite disagreement. They know that real progress happens when people feel safe enough to challenge assumptions, poke holes in half-baked plans, and ask, "Are we sure this is the best way forward?"

Set the Stage for Respectful Debates

Harmony-seeking cultures can be especially hard to navigate. When harmony rules above all else, it can drive resentment, ego battles, or the dreaded meeting that ends with "Let's take this offline" (which, let's be honest, can mean "Let's never speak of this again").

So how do you keep things from slipping into full-blown "passive-aggressive tournament" or "nasty debate" territory? Healthy debate won't just *happen* on its own. You need to create and share norms with your team that encourage open discussion *without* open warfare:

- **Attack ideas, not people.** Debate is about making the work better, not proving who's the smartest. Keep it focused on the problem, not the personalities.

- **Make it a two-way street.** If you're going to challenge an idea, be just as open to having your own ideas challenged. No one gets a free pass.

- **Encourage "challenge culture," not "gotcha culture."** Healthy debate is about curiosity. We're refining here, not tearing down or humiliating.

- **Know when to move on.** If you've debated an idea from every possible angle and still don't have consensus, someone needs to make the call. And when they do? The team moves on together, no holding onto that "I'll just quietly stew in my corner for the next two weeks" energy.

Handling Disagreements Like a Pro

Clearly, not all disagreements are neat and tidy. Sometimes you'll hit a nerve or jangle a power or status structure. Other times someone will dig in their heels like a toddler refusing to leave a bouncy house party. Here's how to keep things from derailing:

1. **Slow it down.** If a debate is getting too heated, pause and recontract with the group. Say, "Let's pause and clarify what we're really debating here." Often people are arguing about different things and don't even realize it.

2. **Frame disagreements as experiments.** Instead of battling over who's right, ask, "How could we test this?" Turning a debate into

an experiment shifts the focus from "Who's winning?" to "What will we learn?"

3. **Watch for power imbalances.** If a junior team member is hesitant to speak up, make an opening for them. Try "I'd love to hear your take on this, Aliyah." If a senior team member is steamrolling, gently redirect: "Let's hear a few other perspectives before we settle on a direction."

4. **End with alignment.** Even if not everyone agrees, you need to leave the debate with a clear path forward. Try "We might not all agree, but here's where we're headed," or "I know we have different views, but here's the plan."

Why Healthy Debate Is the Ultimate Trust Test

A team that debates well is a team that *trusts* well. When people know they can challenge ideas without being labeled "difficult" or "not a team player," they're honest. They push for better solutions.

So the next time you're in a meeting and someone says, "I'm going to push back on that," untense your shoulders. Take a breath, lean in, and remember: this isn't conflict; it's how great teams sharpen their thinking and level up together.

Tip 4: Have 'Em Hazard a Guess

Somewhere along the way, we got it in our heads that certainty equals competence. That if our answer isn't earthquake-proof, we should just keep quiet. But here's another way to look at it: some of the best breakthroughs started as wild guesses. Encouraging your team to make predictions, hypothesize, and—yes—take a guess, isn't reckless. It's creating an environment where people feel permitted to throw ideas out there, even if they aren't fully formed yet. And that first-draft, written-in-pencil place is where innovation lives.

The Magic of an Educated Guess

An educated guess is just like a rough sketch. It might not be the final masterpiece, but it gets everyone moving in the right direction. When people are invited to make forecasts, they engage with the problem more deeply. They connect dots that others might miss. They feel ownership over the outcome. And we've all probably seen it— sometimes the person with the least experience in the room sees the thing everyone else is too close to spot.

Take Netflix, for example. Back in the late 1990s, when Blockbuster was king, a small team at Netflix hazarded a guess: What if people would rather get DVDs in the mail instead of driving to the store? Was it a sure bet? Nope. But they tested it, refined it, and eventually changed how the world watches movies.

Stop Worshipping Certainty

Let's take a little inspiration from Netflix. If you want to build a culture where people aren't afraid to take intellectual risks, make it part of your day-to-day. Not just that, but make it a little enjoyable and fun. Here are some ideas to get you started:

- **Ask, "What's your best guess?" and "What does your crystal ball say?"** Instead of waiting for a perfect answer, invite speculation. The more people flex their prediction muscles, the sharper they get.

- **Reward thinking, not just accuracy.** If only "right" answers are celebrated, people will hesitate to speak up. Acknowledge creative attempts and bold thinking, even when they don't pan out. (Yes, Jason, taco-flavored ice cream *is* interesting, even if it didn't quite catch on.)

- **Play "Wrong Answers Only."** Kick off brainstorming by having people suggest deliberately ridiculous solutions. It lowers the stakes and often leads to surprisingly brilliant ideas.

- **Turn failures into folklore.** Every successful team has its legendary misfires—the ideas that flopped but taught valuable lessons. Share them. Laugh about them. I'll never forget when my team and I tried to streamline our client onboarding process with a 20-page PDF outlining every expectation and detail—and ended up scaring clients off before they even started. This became jokingly known as the *Onboarding Encyclopedia*, but we learned that sometimes less is more!

The Unexpected Win Factor

Some of the best ideas didn't start as sure things. The Post-it Note? A failed attempt at creating a super-strong adhesive. Bubble wrap? Originally meant to be wallpaper. Even microwaves were discovered when a scientist noticed a candy bar melting in his pocket. None of these happened because someone played it safe. They happened because someone took a shot in the dark and followed where it led.

The Power of "I Don't Know"

Let me assure you that, as a leader, you don't need all the answers. In fact, trying to have them all might actually hold your team back. Predictions—whether they turn out right or wrong—are part of what create ownership and sculpt what next. When you sit with uncertainty, it opens up space for creativity and innovation.

So instead of presenting yourself as the one with the answer, invite people's educated guesses instead. Then test hypotheses. The more you do this, the more your team will start to take risks, pitch new ideas, and think bigger.

Tip 5: Name the Unsaid

When something feels *off* in a meeting—unspoken hesitation, a tense silence, an idea that doesn't quite land—it probably is. And if no one names it, it lingers and stalls progress, making it harder for the team to engage honestly.

Psychological safety goes beyond allowing people to speak. You're *inviting* them to. And one of the fastest ways to do that is by surfacing what's left unsaid.

When I had one of my first corporate clients as an entrepreneur, I remember going over the project plan and timeline with them. I could've sworn I saw a flicker of discomfort in their body language—a quick frown, then their eyebrows raised in surprise. I could feel something wasn't right, but I didn't say a word. Instead, I kept going, hoping the discomfort would fade on its own. In the end, they wanted a very different approach that I could've helped raise sooner. Turns out, ignoring things doesn't make the awkwardness vanish. *Who knew?*

Now, I know better. Great leaders don't dodge these moments; they *name* them. By surfacing it, you make room for real conversations and honest feedback.

How to Call It Out *Without* Calling People Out

So how do we say, "Boy, do things feel weird right now"? It's as simple as naming the hesitation you observe with curiosity, not accusation. Examples include:

- "Either this is the best idea ever, or we're all too polite to poke holes in it. Which is it?"
- "I'm sensing some hesitation. What's on your mind, team?"
- "It seems like there's some discomfort with this decision. Let's talk about it."
- "That idea got quiet really fast. What's up?"
- "I can feel us all silently agreeing to ignore the elephant in the room. Should we maybe invite it into the conversation?"

- "I see nodding, but not necessarily agreeing. What's the hesitation?"
- "I get the sense there's a 'but' hanging in the air. Someone help me out here."
- "I feel like we're in 'let's just get through this' mode. What's really going on?"

These statements do two things:

1. They signal that it's *safe* to voice concerns or unspoken thoughts.
2. They remove the burden from team members who might not feel empowered to go against the status quo or speak first.

Unexplained Weirdness? Go First

When leaders name the unsaid, they build a culture of candor. On the other side, when unspoken concerns sit dormant, they harden into disengagement, passive resistance, or quiet resentment.

Help people feel more comfortable speaking up when something isn't working. *Go first*. If a difficult topic is hanging in the air, acknowledge it yourself. "I'll be honest, I have some concerns about X. How are you all feeling about it?" When you go first about a potential red flag, you make it safer for others to follow.

Trust Falls Flat When Silence Rules

When silence takes over, it doesn't mean everything's fine; it usually means people don't feel safe enough to say what they're really thinking. And that's a problem. Naming the tension out loud can feel awkward in the moment, but it's how real trust is built. So the next time you sense hesitation or feel the energy shift in the room, name the thing. Then watch everyone exhale and engage.

Tip 6: Greenlight Risk-Taking and Experimentation

Think of your team for a moment like a group of talented circus acrobats (minus the sparkly leotards, of course). If they're constantly worried about crashing to the ground, they're not going to try the big, daring moves. They'll play it safe, stick to the basics, and never unlock their full potential. But put a safety net beneath them? Suddenly, they're flipping, soaring, and testing the limits of what's possible, attempting and landing routines that once felt impossible. That's exactly what a psychologically safe workplace does for innovation. It provides the net that allows people to take risks, experiment, and push boundaries without fearing career-ending consequences.

What Does a Risk Actually Look Like?

A real risk has a few key characteristics:

- **Uncertainty:** There's no guarantee of success, but there's a clear potential upside.
- **Potential for Growth:** Whether or not it works, the team will learn something valuable.
- **Calculated Exposure:** It's not reckless. It's thought-through, with some safeguards in place.
- **Discomfort:** It pushes people out of their comfort zones but in a way that's manageable.
- **Ownership:** Someone is willing to champion the idea and see it through.

How to Set Your Team Up for Risk-Taking

As a leader, you're facilitating risk-taking one meeting at a time (*think incremental, thoughtful experimentation, rather than BMX Bike flips or*

X Games). Here's how to guide your team through taking smart, meaningful risks:

- **Frame risks as experiments.**

  Instead of asking, "Will this work?" ask, "What can we learn from this?" Shift the focus from success versus failure to discovery. Try saying:

  - *"What's the smallest version of this we can test first?"*
  - *"Let's assume this won't go perfectly. What's our backup plan?"*
  - *"What's one insight we'd gain, even if this doesn't work out?"*

- **Give permission to fail publicly.**

  People need to hear, repeatedly, that failure is an expected part of innovation. Try normalizing risk by saying:

  - *"Let's expect some of our ideas will flop … that's okay."*
  - *"I'd rather see us take a smart risk than play it too safe and miss an opportunity."*
  - *"If this fails, what will we do next? Let's plan for that."*

- **Encourage "AND" mindset.**

  One reason people hesitate to take risks is the fear of making the wrong choice or not having all the answers. The AND mindset, as described by friend and author Shanna Hocking in *One Bold Move a Day*, helps us hold multiple truths at the same time, and it can be a powerful tool when experimenting with new ideas or facing uncertainty.[2]

  Encourage the AND mindset with your team by saying:

  - *"This didn't turn out as expected AND there's still value in what we gained."* (Takeaway: Let's acknowledge setbacks while recognizing lessons).

- *"It's okay if we don't have all the answers yet; let's take the next step forward."* (Takeaway: We can move ahead despite ambiguity).

- *"We can appreciate how far we've come AND still push for what's next."* (Takeaway: We're celebrating progress while staying hungry for improvement).

What Happens When You *Don't* Encourage Risk?

If your team doesn't feel safe to experiment, you'll see:

- **Idea stagnation.** People won't suggest anything new if they think failure will be held against them.

- **Hesitation over action.** Instead of testing and learning, people will wait for *absolute* certainty, slowing progress.

- **A culture of blame.** If every failure results in shaming or finger-pointing, people will focus more on avoiding risk than embracing possibility.

Try This: The "Bold Idea Lab"

Host a monthly "Bold Idea Lab" where team members bring forward bold, risky ideas without needing them to be fully baked. Set the expectation that every idea will either move forward, be reshaped, or be learned from. Adobe does this, through their program "Kickbox," which provides employees with resources and a process for turning their ideas into reality. They're given a kit, a guide, and a small budget to experiment and pitch ideas internally.

Create a culture where risk isn't something to fear but something to navigate thoughtfully and realistically. When people know they won't crash and burn, they'll be willing to take the leaps that lead to real innovation.

Tip 7: Share Airtime

You've probably been in those meetings where the same voices dominate, while others sit in silence, just waiting for it to end. Add to this that's it's often the highest-ranking people in the room who talk the most. It's uncomfortable and, let's be honest, it doesn't get the best results. (Unless your goal is to hear the same three people monologue like they're hosting a podcast no one asked for. *Oof.*) When certain people hog the airtime, you're missing out on truly great insights from others and you're not cultivating the inclusive environment that high-performing teams need to thrive.

The key to unlocking the full potential of your team? It lies in something we all learned in kindergarten: *taking turns*. Dr. Anita Woolley's research on collective intelligence shows that teams perform better when diverse members contribute using equal airtime, not just in terms of quantity, but in the quality of interactions.[3] This sets the stage for higher levels of innovation and problem-solving. So if you want to elevate your leadership, get intentional about equalizing talk time and building a culture of inclusivity.

Why Equal Participation Matters

Think about it: A truly innovative, high-performing team isn't just a collection of individuals working in isolation. (That sounds more like a herd of cats than a unified force!) It's a dynamic, interdependent unit where each person's contribution is recognized and woven into the fabric of the team's success. When everyone has a seat at the table, new ideas surface and fresh perspectives are introduced. Then problems can be solved faster.

Ensuring Everyone's Voice Is Heard

To change a "dominator" speaking norm on your team, try these practices:

1. **Set clear expectations from the start.** Make it clear from the outset that input from everyone is expected and necessary. You might say, "I want to hear from all of you today. Every single one of your perspectives matters." You're priming your team that you're serious about inclusion.

2. **Use round robins to include everyone.** If certain voices dominate, use a structured approach to ensure balance. For example, "Let's go around the room, and each person can share one thought on XYZ." Simple tactic, yes, but ensures everyone gets a chance to speak up, even in larger or more intense meetings.

3. **Facilitate, don't dictate.** As the leader, you want to guide the discussion, not control it. Step back and encourage engagement from others. If you notice someone hasn't contributed yet, prompt them gently: "What do you think about this, Jamie? I'd love to hear your perspective." Encouraging contributions in this way signals that all voices are valued equally.

4. **Reinforce psychological safety.** Team members need to feel safe to speak up, knowing their input won't be ridiculed or dismissed. Reinforce this by saying, "There are no bad ideas here, folks. Let's throw them all out and see what sticks." This kind of environment invites vulnerability and creativity.

5. **Mix up the conversation.** Sometimes, traditional meeting formats can unintentionally reinforce a power dynamic. Mix things up by changing the method of discussion. Try "Let's break into smaller groups for 10 minutes and then regroup to share our thoughts." That unshackles participation from people who might be quieter in a larger group.

Why Inclusivity Drives Results

The deal is this: Sharing airtime comes down to mutual respect. When it's commonplace to hear from everyone, people feel free to share their unique perspectives without the fear of being dismissed or ignored. This is how you move from having basic meetings to high-value discussions with depth.

Make it a priority to share the airtime in your team. Set the tone, facilitate inclusivity, and watch as your team moves from good to great.

Tip 8: Mistakes: Learn and Let Go

I'll be honest: when I make a mistake, my first thought is often "Uh oh, what fresh disaster have I just unleashed?!" My heart rate spikes, and for a moment it feels like I've accidentally hit the delete button on a year's worth of work. I'm sure you've felt that rush of panic, too—the kind that makes you question everything. But then I take a step back and remember a powerful quote by Dr. Amy Edmondson that's posted in my office: "Choose learning over knowing. Look outward and find energy and joy in seeing what you missed."[4]

In that moment, I slowly come back to the idea that mistakes don't have to be devastating. In fact, they're goldmines of growth just waiting to be uncovered.

So how do we shift from panic to progress?

It starts with working on your growth mindset, viewing mistakes as stepping stones for learning and innovation.

The Power of Growth Mindset

A growth mindset is essential for high-performing teams. It acknowledges that intelligence and skills go beyond what we know today; they grow through effort, practice, and—you guessed it—mistakes. Dr. Carol Dweck's research shows that people with a growth mindset are more likely to learn from setbacks and perform at higher levels. So how do we create a culture where mistakes become opportunities?

Shift the Focus from Blame to Learning

When a mistake happens, you want to make a purposeful effort to focus on solutions. That removes fear of failure, and encourages creativity and calculated risks. Here are some concrete ways to make that real:

- **Lead with curiosity over criticism.** As a leader, guide the team; don't criticize when things go wrong. *No one does their best thinking when they feel like they're about to be pounced upon or called to the principal's office.* When an error occurs, ask questions like "What do we think led to this? How can we improve?" That encourages accountability and problem-solving.

- **Normalize failure as part of the process.** Mistakes happen. Make peace with it. Reframe failure as feedback, and encourage experimentation, even if you're unsure. You might say, "We won't always get it perfect, but what can we do differently next time?" This little language shift turns mistakes into opportunities for growth.

- **Emphasize effort over outcome.** Rather than just praising results, recognize effort and the process. Acknowledge the thought and strategy behind trying something new, even if it didn't work. "I appreciate the effort, even if it didn't go as planned. What can we take forward from it?" You're helping the team focus on learning rather than fearing failure.

- **Encourage reflection, not regret.** After a mistake, instead of asking, "Who messed up?" ask, "How can we improve next time?" That grounds the team to own the learning process and empowers them to adjust their approach.

- **Celebrate the learning, not just the successes.** Toast to progress, even if the outcome isn't perfect. You might say, "I'm proud of how we turned that mistake into a learning opportunity. Let's build on this." Success is definitely sweet, but learning something the hard way? That's the stuff that really sticks with us.

Building a Growth-Oriented Culture

When you lead with a growth mindset, you're promoting the belief that *As long as we're learning—and then applying that learning—we're moving in the right direction, even if we took the scenic route to get there.* Encourage your team to take risks, learn quickly from mistakes, and keep moving forward. The more they do, the stronger they'll become. And who knows? That next "failure" might just lead to the breakthrough you've been waiting for.

Tip 9: Not Your Therapist, but Your Trusted Safety Net

I'll be honest: When I think about creating a truly safe space for my team, I'm often torn between two extremes. On one hand, I want them to feel comfortable enough to express themselves genuinely. On the other hand, I know that as much as I want them to feel supported, I'm not their therapist, and I can't solve every personal issue that comes up. It's a delicate balance. You're fostering a space where people can take risks and be vulnerable, without crossing the line into oversharing or becoming a place where productivity gets lost. And that's exactly where psychological safety comes into play.

Smart Filters, Clear Focus

Let's get this out of the way. Psychological safety does not mean anything goes. It's not a free-for-all where employees air every personal grievance or spill all their emotional baggage in the middle of a meeting. It's about finding that sweet spot where people feel safe, not overexposed.

So how do you create a culture where your team can contribute boldly and still feel respected? The key is to provide stability and support. And it may mean defining what's in and out of bounds. Be clear about the types of conversations that are encouraged—feedback, ideas, and challenges—and help people understand when to keep personal topics, well, personal! For example, when things get sidelined into the inappropriate, you might say, "I know we all value transparency, but let's keep things focused on solutions that move us forward."

Lead with Openness and Discernment

As a leader, you're the role model for what personal disclosures are appropriate to share at work. So share what's relevant to the team's goals and the work at hand. If you're struggling with something personal, you can say, "I'm dealing with some personal challenges, but I'm focused on leading us through this. Let me know if there are any ways I can help you stay on track." This acknowledges your humanity, and still sets a direction.

Support Self-Reflection

While your team should feel they can share, oversharing can undermine the culture you're building. (And truthfully, not every personal story needs to make it into a meeting, especially the deep dive into Mike's recent breakup—we can leave the relationship counseling for another time.) Be clear about what kinds of personal disclosures are appropriate at work. For example, "That sounds like something best discussed with your personal support network. Why don't we focus on what we can tackle together here, and you can plan to address X with them?"

Keep It Safe, Not Unruly

Fostering psychological safety creates a space for openness without letting it devolve into oversharing or chaos. Because the thing is, you're actually doing people a disservice if you lead them to think that anything goes at any time.

By setting clear boundaries and modeling a balance between vulnerability and focus, you help people feel supported—without turning your workplace into an emotional venting zone. Keep the equilibrium and you set your team up to feel both safe and empowered to do their best work.

8 The Inclusion Power Moves That Matter

Many leaders genuinely *want* to be inclusive. They tell their teams, "We value all voices" and they might even have a diversity, equity, and inclusion (DEI) statement tucked away somewhere on the company website. But if you ask the people actually experiencing the workplace? The reality can be wildly different.

Real inclusion starts with checking your blind spots and questioning your assumptions, as humbling as that may be. It's staying relentlessly curious about how bias shapes decision-making. *Who* gets hired, mentored, promoted, or trusted with big opportunities—and *how*. Too often, those choices seem objective when they're anything but. Bias is sneaky like that. It disguises itself as "gut instinct," "culture fit," or "the clear best candidate for the job." Truly inclusive leadership means constantly unlearning those defaults and replacing them with better, fairer habits.

Right now there are companies that aren't just pulling back on DEI efforts but are openly dismissing them. Inclusion is being framed in some workplaces as unnecessary, divisive, or even a threat. But leaders who want resilient, future-proof teams can't afford to treat diversity and inclusion like a trend that's in or out of fashion.

They can't pretend either—you'll find no performative allyship here. We're talking about real, *sticky* inclusion, the kind that actually changes the game. The kind that requires stepping beyond what feels comfortable, interrogating long-held beliefs, and bringing a beginner's mindset to the work of building truly equitable, innovative, and high-performing teams.

So if you're ready to move beyond the "diversity pledge" and into power moves that actually matter—welcome in.

Tip 1: Beyond Invitations: Redefining Inclusion

We've all heard the phrase "a seat at the table" as shorthand for inclusion. But sitting in a meeting doesn't mean your voice actually matters there! Extending the invitation might initially open the door, but keeping people engaged and in the room take more. That requires questioning *how* you include, *who* feels safe enough to speak up, and whether your leadership style is making it easier—or harder—for people to show up fully.

An Invitation Without Power Is Just a Spectator Pass

I once sat in an executive leadership meeting at a company notorious for its culture of fear. Technically, I was "included." *But did I feel invited to speak up honestly? To tell their leaders that our survey results showed their employees were miserable?* Nope. I knew the room wasn't built for that kind of open talk. Even so, I shared the hard numbers from their employee (dis)satisfaction survey results, including verbatim employee quotes, and to my lack of surprise, I encountered nothing but resistance.

Being invited into the room does not equal inclusion. Just because you're present doesn't mean you're *invited* to speak freely or challenge the status quo. In fact, in one study conducted with the University of North Colorado Social Research lab, an astonishing 49% of employees surveyed said that they are not regularly asked for their ideas and 40% of respondents said they don't feel confident sharing their ideas.[1]

Who Gets to Shape the Conversation?

Sometimes bias is loud and obvious. Other times, though, it's a whisper in the back of your mind that nudges you to affirm the voices or faces that feel most familiar, most comfortable. You might not *mean* to favor certain perspectives, but if you look at who gets to drive key decisions—who gets heard, who gets interrupted, who gets their ideas championed—you'll probably notice some patterns.

Start paying closer attention. Does the same small circle of people always do the talking? Do you find yourself mentally filtering out voices that challenge your perspective? Real inclusion calls on you to actively *disrupt* these patterns. It's recognizing who's not participating and pushing yourself to seek out the voices that aren't being heard.

Adopt a Beginner's Mindset

The best leaders accept that they need humility: acknowledging they don't have all the answers and that their past experiences aren't a perfect guide for inviting people fully into a moment. Bringing a beginner's mindset shifts your leadership from "I already know what's best" to "What might I not be seeing?" (You can think of this as creating psychological safety for yourself to acknowledge gaps in your knowledge.) It means asking more questions, inviting feedback (and actually listening to it), and recognizing that inclusion isn't a one-and-done checklist. If anything, it's a muscle that needs constant strengthening.

A red flag I've seen again and again? Leaders who assume they've already mastered inclusion tend to make the most exclusionary choices in meetings. And because it's scary for them to consider that they might not know it all, they fail to own, apologize for, or acknowledge exclusion when they should. But the ones who stay open, curious, and self-aware usually learn out loud, in real time. They build the kind of teams where everyone feels safe enough to learn, mess up and own it, and then *know and do better.*

An Ongoing Commitment, Not a Milestone

Inclusion is an *active* practice in every sense. That means paying attention continually to who's getting cut off, who's always being asked to take notes, and who's staying quiet when you know they've got something to say. It means making space for naturally quieter folks, inviting challenge, and showing—through your daily habits, that every voice has weight.

We all have default assumptions about status, including who speaks up and the level of respect we offer them. Your unconscious biases aren't a character flaw but a normal part of your (and everyone's) brain. True leadership is noticing when those assumptions bubble up, and deciding then and there you have a choice about what to do next.

Tip 2: Once You See Unconscious Bias, You Can't Unsee It

Unconscious bias is like an invisible filter you didn't sign up for. No, not the influencer kind you find on Instagram, more like wearing glasses you didn't know you had on, that subtly shape your view of people and situations without you even realizing it.

The great news? And the thing that motivates me to get out of bed and tackle this problem with organizations each day? Once you boost your awareness and start seeing and naming biases, *it's hard to unsee them.* That awareness is the first step toward making more inclusive, intentional decisions that push your team forward. Because now that you see the bias for what it is, you have control over what to do next.

How Bias Shows Up in Your Decisions

We all have unconscious biases. Our brains take shortcuts based on past experiences and social conditioning. The issue arises when those biases quietly influence people's decisions—favoring some, overlooking others, or making assumptions about fit or abilities.

The chart shows common moments to start recognizing where unconscious bias might be creeping into your leadership choices. Each decision is linked to a potential bias, and I share prompts to help check yourself.

Decision Type	Potential Bias	Bias-Checking Prompts
Hiring a new team member	Affinity bias (favoring people like you)	"Am I hiring because they remind me of myself? What's unique about their experience or perspective?"
Promoting an employee	Confirmation bias (favoring existing beliefs)	"Have I considered other feedback? Am I overlooking potential blind spots due to personal bias?"
Delegating projects	Halo effect (one positive trait influencing overall judgment)	"Am I spreading opportunities or recycling the same go-to person? Is there someone else who might benefit?"
Performance reviews	Gender or racial bias (stereotyping)	"Am I using objective criteria? Would this feedback be the same for someone of a different identity?"
Meeting participation	Status quo bias (overvaluing familiar voices)	"Who's talking most, and who's staying quiet? Have I made space for quieter voices?"
Handling conflict	Groupthink (prioritizing consensus)	"Is one opinion dominating? Have I sought alternative perspectives?"
Team feedback	In-group bias (favoring your "inner circle")	"Am I getting feedback from the whole team, not just the people I'm closest to?"

How to Build the Habit of Bias-Checking

Recognizing bias is one thing; addressing it takes commitment. Here's how to turn awareness into action:

- **Pause before acting.** Before making a hiring, promotion, or work assignment decision, pause and ask, "Is there bias here?" This small habit helps avoid quick judgments.

- **Seek diverse perspectives.** Make it a practice to gather input from a wide range of voices, whether for promotions, projects, or meetings.

- **Review past decisions.** Look back at your past decisions and ask, "Did bias play a role?" Learn from them to avoid repeating the same mistakes.

- **Use tech as a partner.** Tools like Microsoft Teams' speaker coach can flag language you're using that might be unintentionally exclusive. Textio can help you write more inclusive job descriptions by flagging gendered language that might turn off certain candidates. Use technology to make sure you're keeping bias in check.

- **Get comfortable with discomfort.** Confronting bias can feel uncomfortable, but discomfort means growth. There's rarely closure or neatness with it. The more you face that, the easier it becomes.

Say It Out Loud and Do It Differently

Once you spot unconscious bias, you can't unsee it, but what you do next matters. Don't underestimate the power of saying "I'd like to pause a moment and consider if this approach is fair," or "It just occurred to me that the deck may be stacked in favor of …" A small intervention like that can spark needed conversation and action.

Tip 3: Be the Ally, Skip the Label

You can look on LinkedIn today and find heaps of profiles that proudly display the headline "Ally." The thing is, this often implies that allyship is a label or something you bestow on yourself. In reality, allyship is earned through action, not so much a button or badge. It requires recognizing the power and clout you have, then using it to lift others up, especially those whose voices are often overlooked or underrepresented.

Think Upstream: Identify the Root Cause of Disparity

It's easy to wonder why certain groups aren't represented in your candidate pool, but here's the difference between a "concerned citizen" and an ally: Allies think upstream. If you see people of color dropping off during the hiring process, dig deeper. The issue is often with the process itself. For example, analyze conversion rates at each stage and compare that with your candidate demographic data. Are there phone screens or panel interviews where candidates are getting filtered out? Allies focus on identifying and addressing systemic biases, not just looking for the immediate fix.

Leaders who only address immediate issues—like interviewing more diverse candidates—miss the bigger picture. Allies challenge the systems that perpetuate exclusion from the start.

Say When It's Not Okay

If you hear a dismissive comment or witness exclusionary behavior in a meeting, use your clout to take a risk. Call it out. Don't let "It's not my place" be the excuse that keeps you frozen. Try saying, "I'm uncomfortable with that comment, Jack. It doesn't align with the culture we're building here." If the person making the comment is senior or in your inner circle, that doesn't make it any less important. In fact, it makes your action even more crucial.

Rethink Who Does the Invisible Labor

Sometimes, these risks may involve confronting microaggressions or subtle biases that might go unnoticed by others. For instance, if you notice that women are always tasked with taking notes in meetings, step in with something like "I've noticed we tend to assign administrative tasks to women, and I want to make sure we're assigning team citizenship tasks fairly. Let's set up a system to make sure everyone takes their turn." When you call out the uncomfortable but necessary things, you're making a stand that signals you prioritize integrity over harmony. You're demonstrating that the injustice is more important than the potential awkwardness or backlash that might come your way.

Redirect Credit When It's Misassigned

Another form of allyship? Making sure credit lands where it's due. If someone restates an idea that was originally shared by another colleague, don't let it slide. You might say, "Yup, that builds on what Maya suggested earlier. I think we should come back to her take on it." It's a subtle way to shift attention back to the originator, without overfocusing on the credit-taker.

Allyship Is a Long Game, Not a One-Off

Being an ally is a process, not an event. It's about continuous learning, unlearning, and doing the hard work every day. Don't expect immediate change, but track the small wins. Celebrate being in learning mode, and keep pushing for more. If your team members feel that your allyship is real, they'll feel valued, more motivated to contribute, and likelier to welcome someone else new in.

Tip 4: Refuse Undeserved Benefits

I'll never forget being interviewed alongside a male author for what was billed as a shared, 50/50 conversation. The setup seemed perfect but as the interview unfolded, it quickly became clear that *he* was being asked the questions. To my surprise, and without missing a beat, he redirected several of the questions to me. Not subtly, not out of obligation, but with intention. "Actually, let's ask Selena to answer that one," he would say, even though the journalist had completely bypassed me. It was an incredible act of allyship. He could have easily leaned into the spotlight, benefiting from the obvious power dynamics at play. Instead, he used his privilege to ensure that I had a chance to shine.

This moment was a clear lesson: Sometimes, the true strength of an ally is in refusing perks or benefits that come your way and choosing to amplify someone else. And, as leaders, we can all adopt this mindset.

Recognize When You're Getting an Unfair Advantage

Ever noticed how perks can be given to some in ways that are invisible to the person benefiting from them? Maybe you're always asked to go first with your project updates. Or perhaps you're given lots of chances to go to offsite events, conferences, or training even though you know others could benefit. The first step in being a true ally is acknowledging that you might be receiving opportunities you haven't necessarily earned—and that others deserve just as much or more.

When you recognize that the pluses you're showered with may not be purely based on merit, you can start to ask yourself some hard questions: *Is this opportunity mine because I truly earned it, or am I being given an unearned advantage here?*

Share the Goodies

When an opportunity comes your way, take a moment to assess if others on your team can partake. Maybe you're the person being invited to attend an important client or prospect meeting. The external folks see you as the face of the work, so you're the one on the calendar invite. What a perfect time to invite in other key players on your team! Maybe they're behind the scenes yet actively contributing to the project. Give them a chance to broaden their knowledge and build relationships, too.

Make Room on the Stage

Inclusion means knowing when to step back and give someone else visibility, too. If you're offered the opportunity to represent your company at an important industry panel or at a conference, consider who else might benefit from that exposure. Instead of taking the spotlight, advocate for a colleague who has been overlooked. You could say, "I think [colleague's name] would be a perfect fit for this panel," or "I want to make sure we're giving others a chance to represent the company, too."

Make the Choice to Lift Others Up

At the end of the day, people will never forget that you used your influence to uplift those who may not have the same advantages. (I know I will never stop admiring and appreciating the ally I mentioned in my story earlier.) So don't let the fear of losing the temporary spotlight hold you back from making room for others. Sometimes the most powerful move is stepping aside.

Tip 5: Receive Others' Stories with Emotional Intelligence (EQ)

Ever plucked up the courage to share something difficult with someone, only for them to respond in a way that stung? One woman I coached shared the upsetting moment a client assumed she was the admin (when she's actually head of marketing). When she told her manager, he brushed it off, saying, "Oh, that happened to Deborah too," followed by "I'm sure it was a joke!"

This is how listening goes wrong—and it's a problem.

High-trust leaders tune in before they weigh in, and not with the passive, nod-along-while-thinking-about-lunch kind of listening. We're talking about emotionally intelligent listening: the kind that validates, deepens trust, and helps people feel seen. If you want a workplace where people feel safe disclosing challenges and lived experiences, you need to master this skill. How you respond when employees share their stories determines whether they'll feel comfortable doing so again.

The Danger of the Knee-Jerk Response

Picture this: An employee shares their experience of being left off important client emails, scrambling for info last-minute. Instead of pausing to absorb, the manager immediately says, "You're overthinking it," or "You're being too sensitive."

Cue the internal eye-roll.

In that moment, the employee learns their perspective isn't valid, not to their boss anyway. The result? They stop raising concerns or leave for another workplace where their contributions are fully recognized.

EQ helps you pause, recognize your reaction, and choose a response that builds connection rather than erodes it.

The Three Pillars of Emotionally Intelligent Listening

Focus on these pillars to become a leader people trust:

- **Empathy: Sitting with someone else's reality**

    Stay with someone in their moment. Don't rush to fix or tidy it up. Resist saying, "That happens to everyone," or "I know how you feel." Unless you've shared the same lived experience, you don't. Instead, try "I'm sorry you had that experience. That sounds really frustrating. Would you be willing to tell me more?"

- **Curiosity: Your best defense against bias**

   Curiosity keeps you from rushing to conclusions. When a team member shares something difficult, don't assume. Ask questions to understand. Instead of thinking, "That can't be right ... they're misreading it," ask, "What did that feel like? How long has this been happening? What would have helped?"

- **Active listening: More than just nodding along**

   Active listening calls for engaging—really engaging. Putting away distractions, making eye contact, and responding intentionally. Instead of "Mm-hmm" or "Got it," try:

   ◆ "I appreciate you trusting me with that."

   ◆ "That must have been really tough. Thank you for sharing."

   ◆ "Thanks for sharing this with me. I want to make sure I understand—are you saying ...?"

The EQ Litmus Test: Would They Open Up to You Again?

Your listening skills are measured by whether people feel comfortable coming to you again. If employees share only surface-level concerns, or stop sharing altogether, reflect on your responses.

Use these MOVES to keep creating a culture where others feel heard, valued, and supported:

- **M**indfulness: Am I fully listening and tuned in before reacting?

- **O**penness: Do I validate others' experiences?

- **V**ulnerability: Do I create a safe space for people to open up?

- **E**mpathy: Am I prioritizing understanding over being right?
- **S**upport: Am I acting on the concerns shared with me?

If you want to build trust and create a workplace where people feel valued, respected, and willing to contribute their best ideas, bring the EQ. The next time someone shares an experience, remember: Your response determines whether you're a leader worth confiding in. Choose wisely.

Tip 6: Remote Work Inclusivity

When most people think of flexibility at work, they picture perks like remote work, flexible hours, and the freedom to tend to an unexpected need. But what's often overlooked is the connection between flexibility and inclusion. So often we think of those as two separate concepts. Yet, they're directly linked. If you want your team to feel truly included, whether they're in the office, at home, or anywhere in between, offer the flexibility to work in ways that honor their unique needs and circumstances.

Why Remote Inclusion Matters (and Why It's Harder Than It Looks)

Imagine trying to complete a scavenger hunt with half the clues missing. That's what it's like for remote workers when they can't engage in spontaneous conversations or subtle workplace rituals. They're missing key pieces that help them fully navigate the team dynamic. Without those cues, they can feel disconnected from the team.

Don't let the "I'm just a Slack message away" mentality fool you either. Communication barriers like time-zone differences and the lack of nonverbal cues can make remote workers feel left out. But the encouraging thing is that with some intention and effort, you can build a strong sense of belonging for everyone on your team.

Start with Regular Check-Ins (Not Just Task Updates)

For some managers, regular check-ins are a rundown of tasks. But they're even more effective when you seize them as an opportunity to build rapport and check in on well-being. These meetings work best when they're two-way conversations, not monologues.

Here are a few ideas to make your check-ins more meaningful:

- **One-on-ones:** These should be scheduled, consistent, and focused on both work and the whole person. If you don't know a thing about their life outside work, you're missing part of the picture.

- **Group check-ins:** Set aside time for team members to discuss things unrelated to work, what they're watching, hobbies, or personal wins. These moments matter.

Virtual Team-Building, Seriously

Virtual team-building doesn't have to be awkward or cheesy, I promise. Get creative and make it fun, so remote workers feel part of the team. Here are a few ways to do it:

- **Virtual happy hours or coffee breaks:** Set up a time for people to connect in a relaxed setting, without an agenda.

- **Online games or challenges:** Virtual escape rooms, trivia, or Pictionary can engage everyone, no matter where they are.

- **Shared experiences:** Send a care package or a team book to discuss. Small gestures like these foster connection and build camaraderie. One of my favorite moments as an unapologetic chocoholic was having a former boss send a chocolate tasting kit to each member of our team so we could taste, compare notes, and have fun while connecting virtually in real time.

Open the Feedback Floodgates

One part of inclusivity involves *what you do* for remote workers. Another is about *how you involve them* in the broader team culture. Ask for direct feedback on the team dynamic, how they're feeling, or anything that could make their experience better. And when they share, take action. Ignoring feedback is the fastest way to break trust but if remote workers see their input leading to positive change, they'll feel a lot more open communicating with you.

Make Them Feel Seen

The most cohesive teams connect beyond tasks—they connect as people. It's easy for remote workers to feel invisible, but regular communication, virtual team-building, and genuine check-ins can help break down those barriers. The more you show up for them, the more included they'll feel.

So the next time you're planning a meeting or project, ask yourself: How am I ensuring that every team member, regardless of location, feels truly part of things? When people feel genuinely invited in, the whole team thrives, no matter the distance.

Tip 7: Creating Inclusive Rituals

Rituals say a lot about a team. They shape interactions, reinforce values, and ensure every voice is heard, regardless of role or background. By embedding inclusive rituals into your team culture, you make sure diversity isn't just acknowledged but actively practiced. These rituals work best when designed with intention, focusing on making sure every team member feels empowered to speak up and contribute, whether it's a storytelling session, rotating meeting facilitators, or regular pulse checks.

Another bonus of making these practices familiar and habitual? The onus isn't always on you to initiate rituals (talk about one less energy "withdrawal" … yes!) because they're baked into your process and they more easily become a lived practice, not a forced add-on.

My friend Eva has a ritual of starting every marketing team meeting by having people share something good that happened personally, something good happening professionally, a challenge, and someone they were grateful for. Week after week these short, consistent shares added up to a full picture of what mattered to each team member and how they are doing.

Why Rituals Matter

Rituals are powerful because they shape how we interact, communicate, and connect. They also help prevent some voices from falling through the cracks by providing continuity and opportunities for everyone to engage in the conversation. Without inclusive rituals, there's a risk that diversity isn't given the attention it deserves— especially when conversations tend to flow around the same voices. Inclusivity rituals, on the other hand, help bring everyone into the fold.

Think Creatively About Extra-Work Rituals

Here's a ritual I bet you're familiar with: the after-work happy hour. Who wouldn't be up for appetizers and drinks to unwind after work? Well, I can think of some: people who don't drink for personal, religious, or medical reasons, and caregivers who need to be there for loved ones after work hours, to name a few. I'm not here to rain on any hang-out-after-work parade, though, but to encourage you to think bigger: What activities could take place that don't only involve alcohol? Or could you let your team off the clock at 3:00 instead of 5:00 for an activity that doesn't conflict with caregiving responsibilities? Varying the kind of activities your team organizes (including virtual events for remote folks) goes a long way toward making everyone feel included.

Learning Together: Building DEI Skills as a Team

Boosting your DEI knowledge isn't as great when it's a solo sport; it should be a shared team experience. Make learning about DEI a ritual. Whether through reading a book together, discussing a podcast, or having regular DEI check-ins, make everyone part of this process.

When DEI learning is built into team rhythms, it sends a powerful message: This isn't a side project or one person's responsibility; it's part of how we grow together. Collective learning invites the good stuff like reflection and a shared language, and it normalizes the discomfort that often comes with confronting bias or gaps in perspective.

Sharing Personal Experiences: The Power of Storytelling

Storytelling is one of the most powerful rituals for inclusivity. Personal stories help team members connect beyond their professional roles. These can be casual sessions where people share personal milestones or experiences that have shaped their perspectives. Storytelling makes diversity feel real. Incorporate it into your team rituals, and you'll see people connect on a deeper level, often interacting more respectfully.

Rituals Create Connection

One company I work with regularly surveys employees on DEI-related topics, and they don't just report general findings—they actively call out red and green flags in the data. If certain groups report feeling less included, or if there's a noticeable discrepancy in satisfaction between different identities, the team discusses it openly in meetings.

This ritual of being open about employee perceptions gives everyone an opportunity to contribute solutions. That makes DEI a dynamic, team-driven process rather than just a set of policies (because no one ever said, "Wow, I just love a good policy").

Inclusive rituals permeate collaboration, ideas, and conversation. If mastery is gained through repetition, then rituals are one of your most powerful tools for culture change.

Tip 8: Audit Your Circle: Who's in Your Network?

Inclusion might start with practices like hiring fairly or equitably managing team dynamics. But here's a just-as-important action we need to take: ongoing self-reflection. And for the sake of *your growth*, let's reflect on your support net: the people you naturally turn to, learn from, and trust. Because the professional circle you keep plays a massive role in shaping your leadership approach. And guess what the hard research shows? Our default inner circles tend to be homogeneous: people who look like us, think like us, and have similar backgrounds. Birds of a feather stick together, right? But here's the problem: This narrows our perspective, limiting the range of experiences and insights that influence how we make decisions and how truly inclusive we are as leaders.

Ready to make inclusion a true part of your leadership style? Let's dive in and audit who's in your network:

- **Inner circle:** These are the three to four people you trust most for professional advice or problem-solving. They're your go-to sounding boards for tough decisions and the ones you rely on for their wisdom and perspective.

- **Core network:** These are the colleagues you collaborate with and depend upon regularly. They're reliable, but not your first call when something hits the fan.

- **Peripheral connections:** These are the broader networks you interact with occasionally, the people you might connect with at industry events or have in your LinkedIn connections, but your interaction with them is more sporadic.

Exercise: Circle Audit

- **Map it out.** Grab a piece of paper and make three circles (as shown here). Write down the names of the people who make up your inner circle, core network, and peripheral connections. Be honest and real with yourself (without judgment).

- **Look for patterns.** Take a look at who's in each ring. Are you seeing variety or are you mostly surrounding yourself with people who think like you, come from similar backgrounds, or share similar experiences?

- **Challenge yourself.** If your inner circle looks like a homogeneous group, you're missing out on diverse perspectives that can help you lead, think, and execute more creatively and inclusively. Don't worry, I'm not asking you to immediately unfriend your entire posse or anything, but to think more strategically and broadly, day by day. Challenge your old default choices when you need a second opinion. Seek out someone who brings a new viewpoint to your work. Whether it's someone from a different department, a younger colleague, or someone from a different demographic, ask them for their thoughts on a challenge you're working on.

- **Invite different voices.** Next time you're working on a tough decision or need fresh ideas, ask a fresh face to be your voice of reason or sounding board. Maybe it's someone you wouldn't normally turn to (like a rising star from your "village" or maybe a software engineer helping the marketing team think differently about customer engagement). The point is to seek out perspectives that challenge your default assumptions and broaden the way you approach problem-solving.

Why does this matter? The more diverse your circle, the sharper your leadership becomes. Stick with the same crew, and you'll stay trapped in a bubble. So step out of your echo chamber. Add some new voices, challenge your assumptions, and watch how it transforms not just your leadership, but your entire team's mindset.

Tip 9: Flip the Default: Make Inclusion a Leadership Standard

Too often, inclusion work is framed as something extra, an initiative that underrepresented employees push forward while leadership "supports" from the sidelines. In many workplaces, these employees are expected to be the faces and primary advocates of DEI. They're asked to lead employee resource groups, educate colleagues, and push for change—on top of their day jobs. And as if that weren't enough, they're usually doing it on their own time, without reward or compensation.

Seriously?!

It's time to flip that default. Inclusion should be a nonnegotiable expectation for leaders, embedded into how they hire, promote, mentor, and make decisions. It's not an add-on; it's part of the job. And did you know that a full 60% of employees *want* to hear leaders speak up on diversity issues?[2]

That means shifting from passive support to active responsibility.

Measure What Matters: Make Inclusion a Leadership KPI

If inclusion is truly a business priority, it should be treated like one. So hold leaders accountable like you would for revenue, retention, or customer satisfaction.

Key questions to assess inclusion as a leadership KPI:

- Are leaders mentoring and sponsoring employees from a diverse range of backgrounds?
- Do your hiring and promotion patterns reflect a commitment to equity?
- Do you ensure decision-making processes include a mix of perspectives?

Companies like Microsoft have tied executive compensation to diversity and inclusion outcomes. You can imagine how—for an employee in particular—that sends a message of commitment and seriousness. When leaders are evaluated and rewarded for progress, they're far more likely to take real action.

Go Beyond Good Intentions: Embed Inclusion into Decision-Making

Think about a leadership team that values inclusion but doesn't act on it. It's a bit like a company that values innovation but never launches a new offering or product. Inclusion needs to be baked into decision-making processes, and if it's lacking, it's time for a decision-making process audit.

Here are some examples of inclusive decision-making in action:

- Making diverse evaluators and perspectives a requirement in hiring and promotion decisions

- Ensuring sponsorship and mentorship opportunities are not just happening informally within existing power networks
- Building inclusive team norms, from who gets the floor in meetings to who is assigned high-visibility projects

Leaders shouldn't rely only on "remembering" to be inclusive; it should be structured into how work gets done.

Treat Inclusion Like Innovation: Experiment, Measure, Improve

We know that inclusion isn't a one-and-done initiative. It's an ongoing process that requires experimentation, iteration, and adaptation. The best leaders approach it like they would any other area of business innovation: they test strategies, collect data, refine their approach, and keep improving. What does this look like in practice?

- **Launch diversity task forces** to tackle specific inclusion challenges (for example, hiring inclusively), and rotate members to infuse new ideas and perspectives.
- **Experiment with reverse mentoring**, where senior leaders learn from underrepresented employees about their experiences.
- **Create "inclusion labs"** where new diversity and inclusion ideas like experimenting with anonymous feedback systems or launching casual, drop-in discussions on topics like male allyship, are tested, analyzed, and refined for effectiveness.

When something doesn't work, adjust it. If a policy isn't moving the needle, refine it and create the 2.0 version. Be the leader who treats inclusion with the same urgency, agility, and strategic thinking as other VIP initiatives.

From Initiative to Expectation

Flipping the default means making inclusion a leadership standard. It calls on you to recognize that real change happens when those with the most influence take responsibility, not when the burden falls on those with the least power.

Let's evolve DEI from a separate initiative to the way business gets done. No extra fluff, just core to the work.

9 Gaining a Higher Viewpoint

As we round out this journey, let's talk about the power of stepping back. It's easy to get caught in the whipped-up frenzy of the day-to-day—email chains, meetings, deadlines—but the real magic of growth happens when you shift your gaze from the details to the horizon. It's just like in those moments where you may have doubted yourself. Maybe you thought you hadn't accomplished enough, but stepping back to see how far you've actually come and how much you've actually achieved probably adjusted (and improved) your reading.

In leadership, the ability to zoom out allows you to see not just what's in front of you today, but what's coming tomorrow. By gaining that higher viewpoint, you become the leader who can navigate complexities, make strategic decisions that serve the long-term vision, and harness the full potential of your team. *The chronic noisiness of small tasks? No thanks. The limits of seeing only what's right in front of you? Nuh-uh.* Learning to think and see bigger will help you spark innovation, challenge norms, and pave the way for growth. This doesn't mean ignoring the small stuff; it means discerning where your time will have the most impact and flying at a higher altitude.

This chapter is all about shifting your perspective, because only when you stop thinking small can you really dream and hit moonshot goals.

When you embrace that elevated view, you can start taking the kind of risks that lead to the next big thing—like investing in a product that no one else sees the potential for, or daring to disrupt an outdated system with a forward-thinking new approach. Ready to step back, breathe, and take in the bigger view? Let's go.

Tip 1: Put Away Your Microscope, Get Out Your Telescope

You're feeling tossed around in a hurricane of emails, Slack messages, and from one urgent task to the next. Sound familiar? Many leaders get stuck in "death by 1,000 tiny emergencies" where they're responding to every little crisis. No wonder it's hard to get a clear vantage point above it all or "think strategy." In fact, one PwC study of 6,000 senior executives revealed that only 8% turned out to be truly *strategic* leaders.[1]

I've certainly been there as an entrepreneur sinking way too much energy into details that ended up not mattering a month later. But great leadership isn't burnished while micromanaging the little stuff. It's only when you see the bigger picture that you can steer the team toward long-term success.

So, right now, let's make a shift from tactical to strategic leadership. To help you get out of the day-to-day and focus on what truly moves the needle, consider these shifts to help you zoom out, think bigger, and lead smarter:

- **From approving every detail to empowering downward decision-making:** Instead of personally reviewing every project, create clear guidelines and trust your team to make the call. To pull this off, you need to let go of control over routine decisions so work can move faster. When leaders empower instead of micromanage, teams become more capable, confident, and efficient.

  Ask yourself: Where am I holding up progress by keeping control? What's one decision I can delegate today?

- **From putting out fires to fireproofing the system:** Tactical leaders spend their days putting out fires. Strategic leaders ask, "Why do these fires keep starting?" So if you're going to tinker and fix something, focus on systems and processes that *prevent* recurring issues, not just quick patches.

  Ask yourself: What's one persistent problem in my team or organization? How can I solve it at the root instead of patching it up?

- **From checking off tasks to aligning actions with vision:** Are you producing things, or are you making progress? Stop measuring productivity by busyness and start asking whether your team's efforts are moving the organization toward its biggest priorities.

  Ask yourself: Do my daily activities support my team's long-term goals? What should I prioritize differently?

- **From inside-out to outside-in:** Sure, great leaders rely on internal knowledge, but they also actively study outside trends, industry shifts, and market forces. Instead of assuming your organization is the whole universe, stay curious about external factors and bring that insight into your decision-making.

  Ask yourself: Am I paying enough attention to external forces and trends? What's one outside insight I can integrate into my strategy this week?

- **From managing people to developing leaders:** Are you known for actively developing people's ability to lead and stretch? If not, invest more energy in coaching and mentoring others to step up. Your success is measured less by how much you personally accomplish, and more by how well you grow the next generation of leaders.

  Ask yourself: Who on my team is ready to take on more responsibility? How can I support their leadership development?

From reacting to change to anticipating what's next: Instead of scrambling to adjust to change, proactive leaders scan the horizon, identify trends, make predictions, and prepare for what's coming. Make it a habit to look beyond today's challenges. For example, add a segment to your ongoing meetings called *What's Next?* where you discuss new disruptions and trends and make sense of them.

Ask yourself: Am I constantly reacting to surprises, or am I preparing for what's ahead? How can I build foresight into my leadership?

Embrace the Bigger Vision

If you're constantly caught up in the small stuff, your leadership impact is limited. How about trying it a new way? Take a step back, scan the bigger picture, and make moves that proactively shape your future. Cement what you learned and make it real right now: What's one tactical habit you need to break, and what's one strategic shift you'll make instead?

Tip 2: Think Two Times Bigger, Even When You Don't Have All the Answers

Here's an unsexy truth about taking risks: You'll never have everything figured out. *Like, never!* The best leaders take bold steps, even when they don't have all the answers. They dream big, explore new ideas, and trust they can navigate the details along the way.

Thinking bigger demands you push yourself and your team out of what's "comfy" and familiar and dare to take on something bolder than you've done before. The key here is to *focus on the direction, not the details*. Don't fret about having everything mapped out. Start with your vision, bring the conviction, and then take the first step.

(And fear not, meticulous planners! The answers will get hammered out along the way.) Consider these practical tips so you can leap past common challenges and think big.

Overcoming the Fear of Uncertainty

Lots of leaders fear making the wrong decision and looking foolish, which can keep them stuck in indecision. But if you wait for everything to be perfectly clear, you might risk something even more ick-worthy: never making progress.

Practical Tip: Start with a "What If" Exercise Sit down with your team and ask, "What if we aimed two times bigger than what we initially planned?" Encourage them to dream without restrictions, no matter how outlandish the ideas. This exercise will get creative juices flowing and help everyone see the potential for something bigger than the current plan.

Accept That Not Having All the Answers Is Okay

As you think bigger, accept that ambiguity—and even some awkwardness—is part of the process. Innovation doesn't happen overnight. It's okay to take risks, make mistakes, and adjust along the way. High-trust, people-focused leaders expect that they'll figure things out as they move forward and embrace discomfort as a sign of growth.

Practical Tip: Develop a "Learn-as-You-Go" Mentality Adopt a mindset of "learn as you go." In practice, that resembles embracing feedback from your team and constantly iterating as you move forward. Remember, setbacks are survivable, and it's okay to pivot when things don't work out. Try committing to stay flexible, keep learning, and be open to new ideas.

Creating Momentum by Moving Forward

The most important thing is to keep moving forward. Once you start taking action, setbacks will happen, and you'll feel frustrated. But it's by maintaining momentum that you refine your vision and uncover new solutions you may not have initially considered.

Practical Tip: Set Bold Milestones Set milestones that seem out of reach but are exciting enough to drive you forward. They don't need to be perfect or fully planned. See them as a series of experiments, even if the full picture isn't clear yet. I remember when I set the goal to write a book in nine months. At first it felt ridiculously ambitious (I had barely finished a draft, let alone a full manuscript!). But I broke it down into bold milestones, like finishing a chapter each week, even when I had no idea if it would all come together. Those milestones kept me focused and motivated when the end goal seemed out of reach. Use these mini markers to keep your team focused and motivated.

Trust the Process

Finally, as my home basketball team, the Philadelphia 76ers, likes to say, "Trust the process." There's real power in your team reaching new heights. Trust that their creativity, energy, and expertise will help fill the gaps. Encourage them to voice their thoughts, no matter how unpolished. The more open you are to their input, the more ideas and solutions will emerge.

Thinking two times bigger calls on you to embrace the unknown and say, "I can handle what comes." Don't wait for the perfect moment or all the answers. Your next big breakthrough is out there waiting for you.

Tip 3: From Project to Cause: Unlocking Your Team's Full Potential

What do the creators of the iPhone, the crew of *Moulin Rouge*, and the Mars Sojourner Rover team have in common? They're examples of hyper-successful teams that smashed records and defied expectations. What set them apart? According to Deloitte's research in *The Cause Effect*, members of these teams weren't just completing work; they were fueled by something bigger: a shared cause that inspired passion and commitment.[2]

So what are you giving your team to work on most days: *a project or a cause?*

If you want to move away from task-driven leadership to a cause-driven approach, here are some tips to help you level up. Keep in mind, though, that the cause effect is for strategic, mission-critical work that aligns with your organization's long-term goals (not just any old one-off project).

- **Define your cause, not just your goal.** Start by defining the cause behind your team's work. Ask: *Why does this matter?* Then go deeper than the surface "Why"—ask why *that* matters. Involve your team in this process. For example, if you worked at a mortgage company, you might find that instead of framing your team's task as "setting up a new loan for first-time home buyers," you'd create more of a cause by positioning it as "Making first-time homebuyers' dreams come true—we're transforming aspirations into reality." Small change, deep impact.

- **Engage emotionally, not just on deliverables.** Feelings of pride, excitement, and ownership drive motivation. Ask yourself: What emotions or elements should the cause evoke? Inspiration? Determination? Trust? People work for more than just a paycheck. They work because they want their efforts to matter. When employees feel emotionally connected to the cause, they'll push through tough times and stay committed, even when challenges arise.

- **Use stories and symbols to win hearts.** Metaphors, stories, and symbols are powerful tools that help your cause resonate deeply. What's a compelling narrative or visual that can make the cause relatable and inspire action? What stories can you tell to make your cause more tangible? For example, if your cause is environmental sustainability, you could use a graphic of a tree blooming or a kid playing by a flowing river, symbols of growth and long-term impact, and tell stories to match. These images inspire action and create a shared understanding of the cause's significance.

- **Connect to the ultimate benefit.** Emotionally connect your team to the ultimate benefit of their work. People are more driven when they see the direct impact of their efforts. How will the world be different because of what your team is doing? Whether it's providing better service or helping others, connect your team's work to real-world benefits. Ask yourself: How can I tie the benefit of this cause to something that truly matters to my team? The more aligned the cause is with their values, the more energized they'll be.

- **Incorporate the cause into everything you do.** Make your cause part of your meetings, communication, and decisions. Make it a regular part of conversations. Infuse it into naming your online files and folders. Remind your team why they're doing what they're doing. When the cause is woven into the everyday, work stops being abstract and drives a sense of meaning and purpose.

Shifting from managing a project to leading a cause will transform your team from a group who happen to be completing tasks to a united force. When everyone's aligned toward a shared mission, their collective energy becomes *a force*. Lead the cause, and watch the momentum build.

Tip 4: Stand Up to Toxic Cultures

Picture yourself walking near a marsh—through a stretch of increasingly tall, thick weeds. Your momentum's slowing as your boots hit constant resistance, and there's a heavy drag that makes every forward movement harder. *This is where your optimism starts to sink with every step.*

Toxic culture can be a lot like that. What starts as a few small "sprigs" of negativity here and there can quickly multiply, dragging down the healthy parts of your organization. And trust me, as someone who's made a career out of walking into tricky dynamics with a notepad and a hopeful heart, I can confirm: Ignoring toxicity only makes it grow weirder. In fact, unhealthy environments tend to grow in silence, fed by tolerance and a lack of confrontation. As a leader, you have the power and the responsibility to clear toxicity. And the thing about this charge? It's ongoing: work that'll never be "done," just like tending to and managing a garden is never technically "finished." Your ongoing commitment to this matters because (and I hate to be the one to say it) those tangles of negativity will always try to resurface.

Recognizing Quieter Toxic Behaviors

Toxicity isn't always shocking or explicit. When it's more subtle, it looks like leaving a person off a meeting invite, undermining their contribution, or casting doubt on their competence. These behaviors may seem small when you're sitting in the conference room, but when they become the norm, they hurt a basic sense of respect. And they may be more pervasive than we think: McKinsey & Co. found in their research that more than 60% of negative workplace outcomes are due to—you guessed it—toxic workplace behavior.[3] Common signs include:

- Passive-aggressive comments that undercut others
- Unflattering gossip that feeds negativity and division

- Dismissing ideas or belittling contributions
- Cliques or exclusion that create division
- Unhealthy competition that stifles collaboration

As you build your awareness in recognizing these signs, congrats—because *that's huge, really.* The next step is naming and acting on the toxicity you see.

Speak Up, Even When It's Uncomfortable

Confronting toxic behavior can be downright awkward; no one enjoys being the "bad cop." But as a leader, you must address it, not with accusations, but with open eyes and a clear voice.

Imagine a meeting where someone makes a snide comment about a team member. Don't wait for it to "blow over." Address it immediately. A simple "We're not here for personal critiques. Let's keep the conversation respectful and focused on solutions" can stop negativity in its tracks.

Here's how to speak up when you witness toxic behavior:

- "Let's focus on the idea, not the person."
- "Let's make sure everyone has a chance to speak."
- "That comment isn't constructive. Let's redirect to solutions."
- "I see some frustration here. Let's work through it constructively."
- "We need to maintain respect, even when we disagree. Let's take a breather."

These simple phrases redirect the conversation and maintain respect. It's about setting the tone for open, respectful, and productive communication.

Hold People Accountable, Starting with Yourself

Toxic behavior is a slippery slope. Small infractions seem easy to overlook, but letting them slide ends up inviting more bad behavior. When you hold yourself and your team to the same high standards, everyone takes responsibility for their actions and impact on others (and accountability isn't seen as punishment).

As a leader, you have a job to nurture respect in every meeting, every conversation, and every interaction. Remind your team that culture is something we need to actively maintain every day *together*.

Ready to Lead the Change?

Standing up to toxic behaviors is an ongoing process, but it's one of the most important things you can do as a leader. It's time to roll up your sleeves, clear away shady behavior, and ensure your culture stays healthy and thriving. Do that—everyone wins.

Tip 5: Prioritize People Over Process

Let's talk about Paul, a team leader at a fast-growing company. He was tasked with rolling out a new customer relationship management (CRM) system across the organization. The goal was to streamline client communications and boost productivity. But Paul faced a challenge: He needed buy-in from his fellow team leads to make the rollout successful.

Paul doubled down on what he knew best: bringing a laser focus to the CRM's mechanics. He wrote specifications and set up training sessions with deadlines. Then he pushed for adoption. He was *certain* the system would work; all he needed was people's compliance.

The result? A whole lot of resistance. As one team lead put it, "He's driving the bus all right, but nobody's on it."

This is what happens when you prioritize process over people. No matter how good the system, it won't succeed unless people feel involved, heard, and respected in the process.

People Over Process: Why It Matters

People want to feel like they matter in the decision-making process. They need to ask questions, voice concerns, and feel like their unique needs are being considered, not brushed aside. But when you focus on process over people, you're saying, "Here's the solution—deal with it," or "We value the work here, but not the people doing it." Trust and buy-in don't come from mandates; they come from conversation and collaboration.

Now, let's look at how Paul could have approached the rollout differently and how you can avoid falling into the same trap:

- **Invite input early.** Before implementing anything, ask for feedback. Socialize your plan with team leads and ask about challenges they face and thoughts on the initiative. The more you involve people in the process early, the more they'll feel invested in its success.

- **Focus on the Why.** Instead of saying "Here's the new CRM," start with why it's happening. Show how the tool benefits *them*, not just the company. When people see how it makes their jobs easier, they'll be more likely to support it.

- **Collaborate on solutions.** People don't want to feel like they're getting a finalized manual with no room for discussion. Include them in the adaptation process. Ask, "What would need to be true to make this feel workable?" Collaborating on solutions makes them part of the change, not just passive recipients.

- **Create space for open dialogue.** Once the CRM was in place, Paul could've kept the conversation going. Regular check-ins allow team leads to provide feedback and raise concerns in an open atmosphere. Then instead of dismissing feedback, Paul could act on it. This shows that you value their input.

Task-Oriented Versus People-Oriented: The Key Difference

Here's a quick table to help you contrast a task-oriented approach (like Paul's) and a people-oriented approach that builds trust and engagement:

Task-Oriented	People-Oriented
Focuses rigidly on outcomes/timelines	Focuses on understanding team needs
Sees change as something to enforce	Sees change as a shared, interdependent process
Pushes compliance without feedback	Encourages open dialogue and input
"Counterattacks" employee resistance	Normalizes and expects employee resistance
Neglects/avoids team concerns or feelings	Actively listens and adapts to feedback
Looks at people as "doers" in the process	Views people as partners in the process

Notice the difference? When you focus on people, you build trust. When you push tasks, you may just alienate the very people you need to succeed. Remember, processes are just tools. *People are what make those tools work.* If you want your team to adopt—and champion—a change, engage them continuously in the process. Do that and you'll turn resisters into supporters.

Tip 6: Coach Yourself Through Change to Lead Others

Ever tried calming a panicked coworker, friend, or family member during a crisis, while you were internally freaking out yourself?

Spoiler alert: It's not that easy, nor is it very convincing! Leading a team through change works the same way. If you're a wreck, acting like there's nothing but turbulence ahead, your team will start bracing for impact too. To guide others through uncertainty, you first need to coach yourself. This means normalizing reactions to change and developing strategies to manage them.

The Brain's Default Setting: Resist, Resist, Resist

Your brain hates change. It sees the unfamiliar as a threat, triggering resistance before you even get a chance to assess if the change is good. Your team's brains are doing the same thing. That's why even small changes can spark negative reactions. So don't pretend change is easy. Acknowledge that resistance is normal, and expect to coach yourself (and your team) through it.

Step One: Get Curious About Your Own Reactions   Before addressing your team's concerns, look at your own. What about this change unsettles you? Are you worried about losing control, failing, or not keeping up? Identifying and labeling these fears helps you manage them, rather than letting them control you. Shifting your perspective from "This change is out of my control" to "I can control how I respond" makes all the difference.

Step Two: Reframe the Narrative   Your mind has likely already assessed worries about the change. Now consciously flip that: What opportunities does this change create? How can you smooth the transition for your team? What's within your control? Changing your perspective from "This shift is being forced on us" to "We're going to make this work" shifts the energy from resistance to possibility.

Step Three: Regulate Before You React   When stress hits, calm your body first:

- Breathe: Remember box breathing from Chapter 6? Inhale for four counts, hold for four, exhale for four. Repeat.
- Pause: Take a moment before reacting to big news.
- Move: A quick walk or stretch can help break the stress loop.

Leading through change requires finding your calm center. Managing the tempo of everything from your breath to your responses shifts you from "I have to react immediately" to "I can always pause, calm my body, and respond thoughtfully."

Step Four: Own Your Communication   Clarity and consistency are key. People don't just want to know what's happening, they want to understand how it affects them. Be direct, transparent, and frequent with updates. If you don't have all the answers, admit it. Trust is built when people feel informed, not kept in the dark. Shifting from "I have to have all the answers" to "I can keep people informed, even in uncertainty" helps build trust.

Step Five: Normalize Discomfort   The awkward in-between phase of change can feel unsettling. Rather than glossing over it, acknowledge it and talk about it. Let your team know it's okay to feel uncertain. After all, change can be disruptive, synonymous with loss, and can even threaten our sense of mastery! Encourage open discussion, create space for venting (within reason), and remind everyone that adapting takes time. Shifting your perspective from "This uncertainty is a problem" to "This is part of the process" helps everyone move forward with confidence.

Lead Yourself First, Then Lead Others   As the high-trust leader, you don't pretend to have all the answers, you approach change with transparency and resilience. When you coach yourself through discomfort, you're better equipped to lead your team with confidence. Who knows? You might come out the other side stronger, wiser, and even excited for what's next.

Tip 7: Curate a Better Inner Playlist

The single biggest leadership change that's fueled my own career? Committing to changing my self-talk. For years, my inner critic was like a DJ stuck on the same bleak track: "You're not good enough. Why are you here? Everyone's about to figure you out." Turns out (shocker!), that's no soundtrack for success. It's mental noise that drowns out clarity and courage.

If you want to show up as a people-centered leader, curating a better inner playlist counts. Here's how to upgrade yours.

Notice the critical voice. First, pay attention to your extreme thinking like "I always …" or "I never …" and when phrases like "I'm failing," "I'm not cut out for this," or "This is a disaster" start looping. These thoughts aren't facts; they're stress-driven responses. Recognizing them is the first step to quieting them.

So make a quick mental "note" to yourself when you hear the critical voice:

- "It seems like I'm putting a ton of pressure on myself right now."
- "Whoa, I'm painting this in pretty dramatic, black-or-white terms."
- "I notice I'm making this feel really big right now."

These moments of recognition interrupt the spiral and create space for a more balanced perspective.

Create an anchor phrase. When stress spikes or self-doubt sneaks in, anchor yourself with a steadying phrase. Leaders I coach repeat:

- "This is hard, but I've handled harder."
- "I'm figuring it out as I go."
- "I don't have to be perfect to be effective."
- "All I need to do is take the next step."

It also helps to bring humor. When the pressure's on, I remind myself, "This isn't the Super Bowl halftime show! No one's expecting me to have fireworks, dancers, a surprise guest, and three outfit changes. Deliver the message and keep it cool." This helps me lighten up and create a more realistic standard. Levity's your friend. Use it to defuse anxiety.

Get some distance. Imagine if your closest friend came to you spiraling with self-doubt. Would you pile on with criticism? Of course not. You'd offer perspective, encouragement, and compassion. Dr. Ethan Cross found that creating psychological distance between you and your self-doubt helps you manage it better; he recommends coaching yourself using your name and "you." So instead of thinking, "I'm terrible at this," try saying, "[Your name], you're learning as you go." Replace "I'll mess this up" with "Actually [Your name], you've prepared, and now it's time to give it your best shot." This language shift helps you view the situation with more objectivity and perspective.

Reframe the stakes. When your inner critic insists, "Everything's riding on this!" zoom out. Ask yourself, "Will this still matter in a week? A month? A year?" Most moments that feel overwhelming now shrink with perspective when you consciously reframe them:

- "Is this truly a make-or-break moment, or is it just another opportunity to learn?"

- "What's the worst-case scenario, and how likely is it to happen?"
- "How would this look if I took a step back and focused on the facts instead of the fear?"

By reinterpreting things, you can lessen the emotional charge and focus on steps you can take now, rather than getting bogged down by what *might* happen.

Your mindset is the soundtrack to your leadership. Realize that, at any time, you have the power to shift from a biting critic to an encouraging, supportive inner coach. Make the commitment, and your inner playlist will start sounding like the wise, capable leader you truly are.

Tip 8: Scale Your Impact

A few years ago, one of my coaching clients, Suzanne—then a director—had the chance to sit down with an SVP who came to town for a quick, unplanned lunch. Despite being frazzled about fitting this into her busy schedule, she was thrilled. This was her shot at exposure, a rare one-on-one opportunity with someone at a higher level. But when the SVP asked at lunch, "What's next for you?" and "Where do you see yourself progressing in the next few years?" Suzanne froze. She hadn't given it thought. She was so caught up in the fast treadmill of everyday tasks, she couldn't answer. The reality hit her: She'd been so busy reacting to the present, she hadn't carved out a bit of space to dream about the future.

This moment was a wake-up call. If, like Suzanne, you're waiting for your perfect moment to envision a bold future, this is your sign to start *now*.

Start by taking some time to reflect and dig deep:

Reflection Prompt	Example
What do you want less of? What's draining your energy or holding you back?	Too many unproductive meetings or tasks that don't align with your goals
What scares you, but also excites you? Lean into that discomfort; it's where growth happens.	Managing a bigger team or stepping into a leadership role that feels intimidating
What would you do if fear didn't get in your way? What's something you'd try if you could be bold and brave?	Manage a high-profile initiative or switch to a different department
What's a leadership skill or habit that excites you to master next? Why is building that skill an important part of your signature leadership style?	Improving decision-making, taking on broader oversight, or developing people
Who do you want to become in the next few years? Not just in your job title, but in your impact and influence. What actions are you taking to become that version of yourself?	Becoming a thought leader who's shaping broader conversations or a leader who champions innovation and change

Don't Let the Day-to-Day Steal Your Vision

So how do you see the bigger picture when the little stuff tries to steal your focus? Lean toward action, manageable and small. Break big dreams into clear steps by asking yourself:

- What's the first step toward developing a skill that will move you forward? (Maybe it's signing up for a course or seeking feedback from a mentor.)

- What challenge have you been avoiding that's waiting for you to step up? (It could be tackling a tough project or giving honest feedback.)

- How can you measure success along the way, even if it's just a small win? (Tracking progress on a new initiative or getting positive feedback from your team.)

Reflect, Adapt, and Keep Growing

Envisioning your future is less about building a rigid plan and more about spotting the next steps that excite and challenge you. Ask yourself: What short-term goal would truly energize me, not just fill a need? Once you've identified it, take one step today to move closer.

And remember, multiplying your impact is a reflective process. Don't be afraid to ask yourself, continually, *Is this building a bridge to where I want to be?* Then make a choice to shift when the answer is no.

Scaling your impact is taking control of your future. Because if you don't, someone else may make assumptions and shape it for you.

Tip 9: Chisel Your Legacy as a Leader

A big part of your legacy is how your people feel on a Sunday evening about Monday morning. Think about it: When your team starts dreading Monday before the weekend's even over, that's not just a bad vibe; it's a relic of your leadership. People may forget the specifics of a project or a quarterly goal, but they'll remember how your leadership made them feel, whether it drained them or motivated them. That's the part they carry forward—the part that lives on.

The Impact You Leave Behind

Some leaders shape a positive legacy through crystal-clear values, intentional behavior, and thoughtful decisions. Others—well, they unintentionally craft a legacy of burnout, distrust, or mediocrity by failing to reflect on their impact.

The takeaway? Don't leave this to chance!

A crucial starting point is to ask: *What do I want people to remember about working with me? What behaviors and values do I want to embody so consistently that they're impossible to forget?*

The Three Leadership Forces You Can't Ignore

Your legacy is built in the everyday moments. There are a few key behaviors that are the "three amigos" of people management, as I like to call them; each has a disproportionate impact on your team. The way you handle tough conversations, respond to mistakes, or celebrate wins leaves a deeper mark than you might realize. Even how you react in your least impressive moments—when you're stressed, frustrated, or blindsided—becomes part of your leadership narrative.

If you want to proactively shape your leadership story, view these moments as the opportunities that they are:

- **When someone fails:** Do you step in with support and guidance, or do you find frustration takes over, questioning how it went wrong?

- **When things go well:** Do you feel the urge to grab the spotlight for yourself, or do you actively highlight the team's contributions, acknowledging their collective effort?

- **When conflict arises:** Are you the leader who listens with curiosity and works to deescalate, or do you find yourself avoiding the discomfort, hoping it resolves on its own?

These everyday choices form the backbone of how people remember you. They shape the trust and respect that define your influence.

Be Known for Something More

The moments that reveal your values and approach speak volumes about the kind of leader you are. If you want to build a legacy you're proud of, that's shaped by intention, not autopilot, you've got to be deliberate about how you show up. Ask yourself:

- **What value(s) do I want to embody every day?** (For example: fairness, courage, learning or curiosity.)

- **What kind of energy do I want to bring to my team?** (Think: calm in chaos, optimism under pressure, or unwavering encouragement.)

- **How will I create opportunities for others to thrive?** (This might include mentoring, sharing the spotlight, spotting potential, or advocating for those who are overlooked.)

Keep It Real

Standout leaders have more than an impressive title. They have a presence that people feel long after they've gone. When your values align with your actions, your legacy takes care of itself. You leave behind a lasting impact that's more than just a memory, it's a movement. So start today. One step. One action. One choice that reflects the leader you want to be. Because you're capable of transforming minds, shifting perspectives, and creating ripples that echo far beyond your time. *That's* the legacy worth building.

NOTES

Chapter 1

1. Hu, J., Zhang, S., Lount, R. B. Jr., and Tepper, B. J. (2023). When leaders heed the lessons of mistakes: Linking leaders' recall of learning from mistakes to expressed humility. *Personnel Psychology* 77: 683–712.

2. Wiens, K. (January 13, 2025). The insidious effects of hurrying. *Harvard Business Review*. Retrieved on March 13, 2025 from https://hbr.org/2025/01/the-insidious-effects-of-hurrying.

3. Rick, V. B., Brandl, C., Knispel, J., et al. (2024). What really bothers us about work interruptions? Investigating the characteristics of work interruptions and their effects on office workers. *Work & Stress* 38 (2): 157–181. https://doi.org/10.1080/02678373.2024.2303527.

Chapter 2

1. American Psychological Association (2023). 2023 Work in America™ Survey. Retrieved March 13, 2025, from https://www.apa.org/pubs/reports/work-in-america/2023-workplace-health-well-being#:~:text=Toxic%20workplaces%20are%20associated%20with,not%20report%20a%20toxic%20workplace.

2. Burris, E., McCune, E., and Klinghoffer, D. (November 17, 2020). When employees speak up, companies win. *MIT Sloan Management Review*. Retrieved March 13, 2025, from https://sloanreview.mit.edu/article/when-employees-speak-up-companies-win/.

3. Diversity matters even more: The case for holistic impact. December 5, 2023. McKinsey & Company. Retrieved March 13, 2025, from https://www.mckinsey.com/featured-insights/diversity-and-inclusion/diversity-matters-even-more-the-case-for-holistic-impact.

4. Phillips, K. W., Liljenquist, K. A., and Neale, M. (2010). Better decisions through diversity, Kellogg School of Management at Northwestern University, Kellogg Insight. Retrieved March 13, 2025, from https://insight.kellogg.northwestern.edu/article/better_decisions_through_diversity.

5. Badal, S. B., and Ott, B. (2015). Delegating: A Huge Management Challenge for Entrepreneurs. Retrieved March 13, 2025, from https://news.gallup.com/businessjournal/182414/delegating-huge-management-challenge-entrepreneurs.aspx.

Chapter 3

1. Gallo, A. January 2, 2024. What Is Active Listening? *Harvard Business Review*. Retrieved March 13, 2025, from https://hbr.org/2024/01/what-is-active-listening.

2. Oppenheimer, D. November 1, 2005. "The Secret Of Impressive Writing? Keep It Plain And Simple." ScienceDaily. Retrieved March 13, 2025, from https://www.sciencedaily.com/releases/2005/10/051031075447.htm.

Chapter 4

1. Li, C. August 26, 2022. The Traditional Employer-Employee Relationship Is Dead. Here's How to Shift to What's Next. LinkedIn online. Retrieved March 13, 2025, from https://www.linkedin.com/pulse/traditional-employer-employee-relationship-dead-heres-charlene-li/.

2. Chang, H.-T., Chou, Y.-J., Liou, J.-W., and Tu, Y.-T. (2016). The effects of perfectionism on innovative behavior and job burnout: team workplace friendship as a moderator, *Personality and Individual Differences* 96, 260–265. ISSN 0191-8869, https://doi.org/10.1016/j.paid.2016.02.088.

3. LinkedIn Learning. Workplace Learning Report 2024. Retrieved March 13, 2025, from https://learning.linkedin.com/content/dam/me/business/en-us/amp/learning-solutions/images/wlr-2024/LinkedIn-Workplace-Learning-Report-2024.pdf.

Chapter 5

1. Kao, W. Emotional signposting: Why you should tell people how to feel. Wes Kao Newsletter. May 22, 2024. Retrieved March 13, 2025, from https://newsletter.weskao.com/p/emotional-signposting.

2. VanEpps, E., Hart, E., and Schweitzer, M.E. (2022). *Dual-promotion: Bragging Better by Promoting Peers.* George Mason University School of Business. https://papers.ssrn.com/sol3/papers.cfm?abstract_id=4128132.

3. Cooperrider, D.L., and Whitney, D. (2005). *Appreciative inquiry: A positive revolution in change.* San Francisco: Berrett-Koehler Publishers.

4. Fredrickson, B.L., and Branigan, C. Positive emotions broaden the scope of attention and thought-action repertoires. *Cognition and Emotion* 19, no. 3 (2005):313–332. https://doi.org/10.1080/02699930441000238. PMID: 21852891; PMCID: PMC3156609.

Chapter 6

1. Laker, B., Pereira, V., Malik, A., and Soga, L. March 9, 2022. Dear Manager, You're Holding Too Many Meetings. Harvard Business Review Online. Retrieved March 13, 2025, from https://hbr.org/2022/03/dear-manager-youre-holding-too-many-meetings.

2. Remskar, M., Western, M.J., and Ainsworth, B. (2024). Mindfulness improves psychological health and supports health behaviour cognitions: Evidence from a pragmatic RCT of a digital mindfulness-based intervention. *British Journal of Health Psychology* 29 (4): 1031–1048. https://doi.org/10.1111/bjhp.12745.

3. Enboarder. October 11, 2022. How much is human connection really worth? Retrieved on March 13, 2025 from https://info.enboarder.com/hubfs/PDF/Human-Connections-Workplace-Summary.pdf.

4. The High Price of Analyzing the Business Implications of an Under-Vacationed Workforce. Project Time Off. US Travel Association. Retrieved March 13, 2025, from chrome-extension://efaidnbmnnnibpcajpcglclefindmkaj/https://www.ustravel.org/sites/default/files/media_root/document/High_Price-of_Silence_FINAL.pdf.

Chapter 7

1. Lin, W., Koopmann, J., and Wang, M. (2020). How does workplace helping behavior step up or slack off? Integrating enrichment-based and depletion-based perspectives. *Journal of Management* 46: 3385–3413.

2. Hocking, S.A. (2023). *One Bold Move a Day: Meaningful Actions Women Can Take to Fulfill Their Leadership and Career Potential.* New York: McGraw Hill.

3. Woolley, A. W., Aggarwal, I., and Malone, T. W. (2015). Collective intelligence and group performance. *Current Directions in Psychological Science* 24(6): 420–424. https://doi.org/10.1177/0963721415599543.

4. Edmondson, A. C. (2023). *Right Kind of Wrong: The Science of Failing Well.* New York, NY: Atria Books.

Chapter 8

1. Hurt, K., and Dye, D. *Courageous Cultures: How to Build Teams of Micro-Innovators, Problem Solvers, and Customer Advocates.* New York: HarperCollins, 2022.

2. Why Is Diversity and Inclusion Important? Diversity in the workplace statistics. LinkedIn Learning. Retrieved March 13, 2025, from https://learning.linkedin.com/resources/learning-culture/diversity-workplace-statistics-dei-importance.

Chapter 9

1. Leitch, J., Lancefield, D., and Dawson, M. May 18, 2016. 10 principles of strategic leadership: How to develop and retain

leaders who can guide your organization through times of fundamental change. PwC: Strategy + Business, Autumn 2016 / Issue 84. Retrieved March 13, 2025, from https://www.strategy-business.com/article/10-Principles-of-Strategic-Leadership#:~: text=It's%20in%20the%20do%2Dor,the%20capacity%20for% 20strategic%20leadership.

2. The Cause Effect. 2016. Deloitte. Retrieved March 13, 2025, from https://www2.deloitte.com/content/dam/Deloitte/us/ Documents/process-and-operations/us-the-cause-effect-book.pdf.

3. Toxic Exodus. July 26, 2022. McKinsey & Company. Retrieved March 13, 2025, from https://www.mckinsey.com/featured-insights/sustainable-inclusive-growth/charts/toxic-exodus.

ACKNOWLEDGMENTS

To my husband, Geoff, and my twins, Leo and Noelle—thank you for your endless patience, quick wit, and ability to pull me out of a writing spiral with a well-placed joke or a plate of ginger cookies (bonus points for both at once). You three are my favorite distraction and my greatest joy.

To my mom, Genevieve—thank you for being my first and most steadfast example of leadership. Your wisdom, encouragement, and constant belief in me have shaped so much of who I am. And for every reminder to rest (that I probably ignored), consider this my official, public apology. You were right about everything. I'm finally starting to listen.

I owe a huge thanks to my Wiley editor, Zach Schisgal, and editorial assistant, Amanda Pyne, for seeing the vision for *Quick Leadership* and helping to bring it to life. To my developmental editor, Julie Kerr, and managing editor, Michelle Hacker—thank you for sharpening my words while preserving my voice. Your edits made every chapter smarter, tighter, and significantly less likely to include three metaphors in one sentence (you were right). And to my agent, Erin Niumata, thank you for championing this book from day one, for your fierce advocacy, sharp guidance, and unwavering belief that this message mattered. You've been a steady hand and a true partner in every sense.

A heartfelt thanks to my inner circle—Chelsea Wiersma, Madyn Singh, and Eva Jannotta—for being the ones I turn to for big ideas, bold moves, and reality checks. Thank you for championing this book from day one and reminding me (frequently) to think big. What a concept!

To my amazing network of thinkers, doers, and occasional daydreamers—including Simone Ahuja, Jodi Glickman, Ruchika Tulshyan, Nihar Chayya, Sohee Jun, and Shanna Hocking—thank you for the brainstorming sessions, tough love, and laughter. Leadership is way easier (and significantly more fun) when you've got a solid crew—and mine's basically the Avengers, minus the spandex.

Finally, to every manager who has ever wondered, *Am I doing this right?*—who has faced hard conversations with a deep breath and shaky confidence, or who has lost sleep over how to truly support their people—this book is for you. I hope it gives you a few answers, a lot of reassurance, and permission to lead like a real person, not a robot in a blazer.

ABOUT THE AUTHOR

Selena Rezvani is a recognized consultant, speaker, and author on leadership. She's coached and taught some of the brightest minds in business, and has spoken at Microsoft, the World Bank, Under Armour, HP, Pfizer, Harvard University, Society of Women Engineers, and many others. She also consults to corporate management teams, using diagnostic assessments to help them advance workplace culture.

Selena is the author of three leadership books: *The Wall Street Journal* bestseller *Quick Confidence: Be Authentic, Create Connections, and Make Bold Bets on Yourself* (Wiley 2023), as well as *Pushback: How Smart Women Ask—and Stand Up—for What They Want* (Jossey-Bass, 2012) and *The Next Generation of Women Leaders* (Praeger, 2009). Selena's experience in leadership and career management makes her a frequent spokesperson and resource for news media. Her advice has been featured in *Harvard Business Review, The Los Angeles Times, The Wall Street Journal, Forbes,* Oprah.com, and ABC and NBC television. Selena is also a popular content creator, making daily video content on leadership for her following of over 500,000 people across platforms, and in 2021 Fast Company named her a Top Career Creator. In 2019, Selena's TEDx Talk on gender bias was recognized with the Croly Journalism award. Today, she writes on leadership for NBC's *Know Your Value.*

Over the last several years, Selena has launched over 25 popular online courses on LinkedIn Learning, which have been viewed by a million learners. She has BS and master of social work degrees from New York University, and an MBA from Johns Hopkins University. Selena lives in Philadelphia with her husband, Geoff, and 12-year-old boy-girl twins. For more information, visit www.selenarezvani.com.

INDEX

Lead like someone people want to follow

Visit SelenaRezvani.com or scan the QR code to access:

- Free book club resources
- Exclusive videos and extra tips
- Blog resources for teams, managers, and HR pros
- Speaking, coaching, and bulk book info
- And more ways to lead with guts, not guesswork

The future of leadership is bold, human, and starts with you.

SelenaRezvani.com